SMART CHOICES
THAT WILL CHANGE
YOUR LIFE

ALSO BY HATTIE HILL

Women Who Carry Their Men

SMART CHOICES
THAT WILL CHANGE
YOUR LIFE

Hattie Hill

St. Martin's Griffin ★ New York

Designed by Marc Burkhardt

www.stmartins.com

Library of Congress Cataloging-in-Publication Data

Hill, Hattie.
    Smart choices that will change your life / by Hattie Hill.
      p.   cm.
    ISBN 0-312-25466-0
    1. Man-woman relationships—United States.   2. Women—Psychology.
   3. Women—Attitudes.   I. Title.
   HQ801.H48 1998
   306.7—dc21
                                                      97-27169
                                                       CIP

First published in the United States under the title *Smart Women, Smart Choices* by Golden Books, Golden Books Publishing Co., Inc.

First St. Martin's Griffin Edition: June 2000

10 9 8 7 6 5 4 3 2 1

To my mom, Carrie Flowers;

my sisters, Bernice, Dorothy, Glenda, Phyllis, Jennifer,
and (sister seven) Deloris;

and to my niece, Raven,

and the next generation of smart women

ACKNOWLEDGMENTS

None of these words would have made it to the page without the encouragement
and support of many wonderful people.

I am grateful:

To my family, who shared life experiences with me and helped to shape the
person I am today; and to my extended family, the New Hope Community, and my
friends who allowed me to stretch and grow.

To writers Shirley Schwaller and Beverly Forte, Ph.D., whose patience and
guidance helped bring this book out of my head and onto the page; to Les Brown
for his advice on this project; to Gladys Knight for her contribution and pushing
me to network; and to my agent, Jan Miller, who for several years patiently
encouraged me to write this book.

To the special women who helped to breathe life into this book—
thanks for sharing yourselves.

To my "safe circle" of friends who pushed me constantly, and to my New Year's
Eve gang who challenged me to finish this book: Rita, Rochelle, Velma, and Linda.

Above all, thanks to the many women around the world who have touched my
life. You made a difference. To God be the glory.

CONTENTS

PART II: SMART CHOICES

FOREWORD

This book is long overdue. I know from personal experience what happens when a woman takes the financial and emotional lead in a relationship, whether it be with a husband, business associate, or family member. I've been there. Done that. And I bought the T-shirt.

My friend Hattie Hill has been there too. Like many of us, Hattie has learned that we must make choices—wise choices—if we are to live our dreams.

For example, powerful women often have a tough time with relationships. A successful life or manageable career for these women often hinges on striking a balance between their need to achieve and the demands of their relationships. Most of us were unprepared for the changes success would bring to our lives, but, particularly, to our relationships. As I heard one of my friends say one evening, "All the world's a stage, and most of us are desperately unrehearsed."

As I read this book, I was struck by how much I identified with the women who are talking about the frustrations and resentments of carrying. There are so many issues they had to deal with: the surprise of finding themselves the primary provider; the subtle issues of control that take over as their career soars; the high expectations of these women and their willingness to take on most of the responsibility in order to see those expectations fulfilled; the willingness of their husbands and family members to let themselves be carried as they, in turn, abdicate responsibilities; and, finally, destruction of their relationships as these women burned out.

I know how many hours of effort and hard work are required to give a first-class performance. But I always assumed that when I fell in love, I'd stay in love, just as I assumed that when I grew up, I'd be grown up. But being in love and growing up take just as much effort as being elected to the Rock and Roll Hall of Fame. I believe in setting goals. Being in the Rock and Roll Hall of Fame was one goal the Pips and I set and achieved. But it wasn't until much later in life that I realized relationships take the same "goal setting," the same effort based on sound choices, as my career.

I was so glad to see the solutions offered by *Smart Choices That Will Change Your Life*. While struggling under the weight of carrying someone, it it hard to see solutions. It is not natural for women to dominate any more than it is natural, believe it or not, for men to dominate. As human beings, we are meant to collaborate—to work together, to grow together, to play together, and to laugh together.

Gladys Knight

PREFACE

The idea for this book emerged from my experience in teaching women's programs. I heard over and over the difficulty working women were having reconciling their original expectations of marriage and career with the challenging new realities of today's world. I kept hearing from successful career women who were now shouldering a disproportionate share of the load. They were, in effect, carrying their men, carrying their families, even carrying their business associates and coworkers.

For women carrying their men, it was a hush-hush issue. The women were embarrassed, and, in most cases, never shared their situation with their peers or coworkers. They certainly never spoke of it in a group presentation. Only when we had occasion to be alone did they bring it up. Often, women would come up to me after a presentation and say, "Can I speak with you privately?" Each of them thought they were the only person dealing with the confusion and frustration of finding themselves head of the household.

For most, the situation presented difficulties they never expected when they first married. The men resented their wives' success. The wives couldn't understand how they'd succeeded while the men got left behind. Both parties were unhappy.

After hearing so many stories, I realized we were dealing with a common occurrence that was simply not talked about, in much the same way as women are often too embarrassed (or afraid) to talk about domestic violence in their homes.

Whoa! I thought. Here is something that needs airing—not only to help other women, but also to allow us to help ourselves.

I use the word "us," because I am included, too. In the midst of my fast-growing business, my relationship with my husband underwent tremendous changes. I was moving too fast to see those changes. Only after hearing from so many other women did I wake up and realize I had also become a woman who carries. By then, it was too late to save our once-happy relationship. Only after my divorce did I stop long enough to wonder if the outcome might have been different if I had been better informed of the warning signs of carrying a spouse.

As I began to discuss and explore this growing phenomenon with other women, we discovered that carrying went deeper than our spousal relationships. We discovered our tendency to carry the principal burden for other family members, for friends, even for coworkers. Smart, high-achieving women, it appeared, often took on more and more responsibilities. They thought they were *caring*—being good wives, daughters, mothers, sisters, friends, and professionals.

Caring turns into *carrying* when we take on the responsibilities of others. The difference between caring and carrying is a fine line, not always easily distinguishable even by smart, compassionate people. The results are more obvious. Burnout, resentment, and frustration result from adding layers and layers of responsibilities. Resentment and anger surface in the people being carried, too, as their willingness to turn over responsibilities produces a loss of their own autonomy and independence.

This book explores the lives of women who have developed such destructive relationships. I thought sharing their solutions and new choices would benefit us all.

This book is not a scientific study. It is a collage of experiences from women across the country. The names of the women have been changed, and their situations altered to protect their anonymity, but they represent many of us. It is not just the executive woman in the corner office who is carrying others. It might be the bank teller, the telephone customer-service representative, the checkout clerk. We are everywhere.

Nor is this book just a woman's gripe session. We are turning the mirror on ourselves to see what role we played. How did we get into this situation? What choices did we make? What can we do differently next time?

We must do this—take an in-depth look at ourselves—if we want to stop the cycle of carrying. Otherwise, we can expect it to occur again and again in an endless spiral.

So, we invite you into our living rooms for a conversation—with smart women who learned to make smart choices.

PART I
SMART WOMEN

Chapter 1
What Happens to Smart Women?

Superwoman is a myth, not reality. No longer is "stronger, faster, better" the formula for success in living a meaningful life. Women must discover a new way of meeting the overwhelming demands of modern times. And that requires new choices.

There is strong anecdotal evidence, however, that many women, regardless of how intelligent they may be, have not gotten the word. A host of women in today's world are shouldering a disproportionate share of the load—financial and emotional—both at home and at work. I call it *carrying.*

Over and over in my speaking and training sessions, both nationally and internationally, women approach me about the stress they are under because they are carrying the lion's share of the responsibility in their relationships, whether those relationships involve a husband, co-workers, or families. Let's listen:

What I find challenging is that people often put me on a pedestal. No one objects to my being a good biochemist—as long as I have dinner on the table by

6:30 P.M., *the kids' gym clothes washed for the next day, my nails polished and my hair cut, and I stay pleasant and unassertive.*

I almost never get home before 11 P.M. I'm always the last to leave the office. I tell people my family comes first, but my actions say otherwise. Sometimes the very marrow of my bones aches, but I don't know how to do less. It seems only I can do the job and do it right.

I control all the financial decisions at home. My husband is no good with money. If I give the checkbook to him, the bills are late, the credit cards maxed out. And as long as he gets to play in his darkroom, he really doesn't care what color the couch is—or even if we have one. He's disengaged and I'm on overload.

"Anything worth doing is worth doing frantically" is my motto. I take on more than I can handle because when I hand it over to someone else, whether it is my family or coworkers, I end up going back and fixing it later. I've given up on anyone meeting my expectations.

These women are responsible, caring individuals. Their gut instinct is to say, "Yes," when they sense a need. "I can do that," they reason, "and that . . . and that . . . and that." They begin to see themselves as their own superhero, able to handle home, family, work, and friends—to do it all! They not only embrace new challenges but volunteer to take on new responsibilities way beyond what is expected of them.

They carry other people's responsibilities when those people fall short of meeting their expectations. Only someone with supernatural powers could execute the responsibilities they have accepted as their own.

Nowhere is this issue more sensitive than in a marriage. Most of us when we marry visualize a relationship in which each partner supports the other. One spouse might be a step ahead at one point, and another might be two steps ahead at another. On occasion, one or the other might need additional emotional support to weather life's storms. Basically, though, in an ideal relationship, the two share the load. But for many of us, that is not what happens.

Instead, many of us find ourselves way ahead of our husbands, both financially and in other aspects. In fact, a 1996 article in *Fortune* magazine pointed out that 29 percent of working wives—10.2 million women—make more than their husbands. Among upper-income women, the percentage is much higher. Three-fourths of women executives at Fortune 1,000 companies outearn their husbands. This shift in economic power is so sensitive that the women do not talk about it, even with their spouses or their friends. Instead, as the gap widens, the women find themselves shoring up their husbands' egos and taking on increasing responsibilities in all aspects of their lives. Before long, often without realizing what is happening, they find themselves shouldering the full weight of the financial and emotional loads. They are carrying.

Carrying, however, is not limited to spousal relationships. These same women often carry more than their share of responsibilities at work, with friends, and in the extended family. The same characteristics that cause them to take on increasing responsibility for their marriage also lead them to carry others in all areas of their lives.

Jessica, a legal secretary, is an example of a single parent who has picked up responsibility for a friend. Four years ago, she bought a house, a "fixer-upper." For the next two years, she painted and wallpapered, redid the plumbing, and shored up the house until it was the model home in her modest neighborhood.

In the meantime, Jessica met Rachel, a single mom at Jessica's church. Jessica was aware that her new friend was barely making ends meet financially. Since Jessica lived alone in her three-bedroom home, she felt compelled at one particularly dark moment in her friend's financial life to offer Rachel and her two children the opportunity to move in for reduced rent. In return, Rachel would help with household maintenance, cooking, and keeping up the yard.

It worked fine for a few months. Rachel missed a couple of months' rent, but Jessica understood why and wasn't bothered by it. She was just glad she was there to help. But Rachel found a new love and the relationship changed dramatically. Jessica found herself baby-sitting almost every evening. She wasn't really bothered by this at first. Instead, she felt that she offered a perspective on life and help to the children in ways that Rachel couldn't provide.

Other changes took place. Rachel wasn't there to cook, clean, or help anymore. Nor did her financial situation improve. Rachel continued to be strapped for cash. She wasn't saving money as Jessica had hoped would happen when she first made the offer to help. Jessica was carrying Rachel and her two children.

Caring versus Carrying

We need to differentiate between *caring* and *carrying*. Webster's dictionary defines carry as "to move while supporting, convey, transport" and "to bear the weight or burden." Both definitions fit the situations described in this book. Carrying is different from caring. It far exceeds the attention we lovingly give to those around us. But it isn't always easy to tell the difference. Consider the following scenarios:

It's 10 P.M. and twelve-year-old Ian is in tears. He has a book report due tomorrow, he's tired, and he has, quite frankly, lost it. His mother offers to type while he dictates the report. In the process, she also asks questions and guides him in thinking through what to say. Is she caring or carrying?

Ruth, manager of the diversity department, and Vicky, the manager of the finance department, need to complete a joint budget for the corporate office by Monday morning. They are behind schedule and decide to work on the weekend. Two hours into the job on Saturday morning, Ruth announces that she must leave. Vicky stays until 8 P.M. finishing the budget. Is she caring or carrying?

Patricia has a twenty-five-year-old son living at home not paying rent. Is she caring or carrying?

For the last three years, Janet has filled out her mother's insurance and Medicare forms. Is she caring or carrying?

Susie is spending every evening after the children are in bed designing a new catalog for her husband's business. Is she caring or carrying?

The answer for each of these scenarios is, it depends. The line between caring and carrying can seem hazy. Consider the first scenario, in which Ian, a sixth grader, is panicked over a book report due the next morning. If he has a legitimate reason why the book report is not done (he's been ill, family emergencies have sidetracked the normal routine, etc.), then his mother's help is an act of caring. But if Ian routinely waits until the last second to begin his assignments and counts on Mom to bail him out, then Mom is carrying.

In the second scenario, if Ruth must leave to take care of a family emergency, then Vicky's willingness to stay and finish the job is caring. If, however, Ruth plans to catch an early afternoon movie with friends, and she knows from experience that Vicky can be counted on to complete the job, then Vicky is carrying.

The same is true of Patricia's son living at home. If her adult son chooses to live at her home so that he can buy an expensive car, she is carrying. If her son has an entry-level job and college debts to pay off, and Patricia is allowing him to live at home for a year to pay off those debts, she is caring.

See the difference? If Janet's mother is unable for medical or mental reasons to fill out her forms, then Janet's doing so for her is caring. If Janet is simply playing to her mother's unwillingness to learn, then she is carrying. If Susie and her husband are both engaged in designing the catalog, then Susie's willingness to help is caring. If her husband is watching the David Letterman show while she works . . . well, you get the drift.

Caring is an act of love. Carrying is a misuse of love.

Smart women often carry because they are smart. They know they can do the job more easily, better, and faster, and believe they are helping the other person. But by taking on the responsibility of others, these highly capable women rob these people of their right to choose. What began as a loving gift transforms into a heavy burden, as acts of love become expected tasks. Carrying changes friends and family into baggage.

Soon the carriers are dragging a bigger load than they can comfortably bear. Often, at some turning point, they run out of gas. And not only has the person being carried been stripped of his or her life choices, but so has the person who carries, as she becomes overcommitted and unable to do it all. It's a lose-lose deal.

There are signals along the way that something is awry. But too frequently smart women keep shouldering a bigger and bigger load until some self-shattering event or series of events hits them hard. I call it a "two-by-four" experience because it's like being hit on the head with a heavy board. It gets your attention. Then the women who carry finally see what's happening and ask themselves in shock, "What am I doing here?" They realize they have made self-destructive choices. Now they must make new ones.

Implementing those choices is not always easy. Not only must you change your own behavior, but you must deal with the ripples that behavior change makes on others. Sometimes those ripples seem like tidal waves. As you go through change, you meet resistance. Learning how to deal with this is an important part of making smart choices.

My own story is typical of a woman who carries.

Hattie: No Excuses

My early childhood was the embryonic training ground for believing I could do it all. One of the first lessons I learned was that no excuse worked when I didn't complete a task. I was the fourth of six daughters raised by a single mom in rural Arkansas. We were poor, my mom worked a factory job, and we raised okra to supplement our income. My mom was both father and mother, and she did both jobs admirably. The neighbors in our small community and church chipped in, keeping an eye on us and reinforcing Mom's strong sense of right and wrong when she wasn't there. Mom loved and nurtured us, but she also doled out discipline with a hard hand. "No excuses" was her motto.

If I told her I didn't feel well, she would say, "Go on to school. You'll feel better after a while." Once I was at school I had no way to get home so, regardless of how I felt, I had to make it through the day.

When our car had a flat tire, Mom would hop out and change it herself, even if there were three men standing around. My great-grandmother, my aunt, and my cousin were just like her. I came from a family of women who *got things done.*

This approach served me well through high school and college. By high school I, too, was taking charge. My biggest desire was to get off the farm. I worked in the field beside our small house and watched the planes fly overhead.

"Some day, I'm going where those planes are going," I vowed. That was my dream.

The first step was escaping our small town. I joined every school organization that took a bus trip to anywhere, just so I could travel.

The second step was education. I knew education was my real ticket to the world outside rural Arkansas. Mom didn't have the money for college, so, in addition to grants and loans for low-income students, I applied for every scholarship from the high school counselor's files that sounded remotely achievable. I garnered enough money for my freshman year at college that more than paid my way. In fact, I lived better than some of my more affluent friends.

By the time I graduated with a master's degree in counseling and psychology, my expectations of myself and others were soaring. I felt I could do anything. These expectations took me farther down the path to being a carrier.

I took a job in a small town outside Houston. I met a wonderful man, caring and responsible. But I put off his proposal of marriage because I wanted to live in Dallas, where I saw my best career opportunities.

He found a position in Dallas a few months later, and we were married. We were buzzing the first few years. We had comfortable jobs, he with a major firm, me with the state. We were partners. We were friends. We had fun—lots of fun.

And then I jumped on the really fast track. Bored with my job and needing a challenge, I started a part-time training and consulting business from our home. My husband was very supportive. The first all-day seminar I gave, he called me at noon, and said, "I've been thinking about you all morning. I'm praying for you and with you." He was great! And the seminar went great!

The business took off like a flash, far exceeding our expectations. I was soon making money, lots of money. I quit my state job. We bought a bigger house, nicer cars, and I began to accumulate furnishings, china, and crystal—nice things I did not have growing up.

Then a subtle shift occurred. I began to take control. Taking control saved valuable time. It reduced stress if I did whatever task needed to be done, because I was assured it would be done right. I even promoted the illusion of helping others by doing it myself.

For a while I was really soaring. All my childhood dreams of traveling were being fulfilled. I had business throughout the United States and overseas in South Africa, Europe, and the Caribbean. As the pace of my life picked up, I began to make quick decisions without the input of my husband. Pretty soon, I was making all of the decisions, including spending our leisure time with my new, exciting friends.

The result? My husband and I grew distant. What I call The Airport Test should have been a clue. When I first started traveling, he would meet me at the gate, give me a big hug, smile, and ask me how the program went. After a while he began to pick me up at the curb after I retrieved my luggage. Finally, he suggested I leave my own car at the airport.

My genuinely nice, professional husband was also genuinely unhappy. So was I. Finally, after another few years of trying, and soul-searching, we split up. Divorce wasn't easy for either of us because of our religious backgrounds. There was no adultery, or violence, or any of the usual, valid reasons for divorce.

Only in retrospect did I have time to reflect and wonder if the scenario might have played out differently. What role did I play? What role did he play? Why were we not taking turns leading versus my carrying all the time? What might I have done differently? What might we have done differently? What do I need to know before I become romantically involved again? Why was I making all the decisions? Was it money or something else? Was it me, him, or us? I never intended to carry. It started in small ways and grew. What choices could have made a difference for both of us?

As I re-examined our marriage, I realized I was carrying. But it wasn't just my marriage. I was carrying a coworker, several family members, and a friend. A whole parade was leaning on me. When did I cross the line from a smart, independent woman to one whose cape was so weighted with others' concerns that I could no longer fly? In fact, I could barely walk.

I wasn't the only one asking these questions. I heard them from countless other women.

How does this happen to smart women? How do we let it happen to us? What is the role we play and how do we end this cycle of carrying and find new meaning in our lives?

This book shares the stories of seven women who traveled such a journey of discovery. They represent all of us.

The next chapter introduces these women. They come from a

variety of backgrounds—geographic, socioeconomic, and ethnic. All work. Some are executives. Some are staff. Some are entrepreneurs. Some are mothers. Some are not. Some are married. Some are not. Some carried their husbands, some their grown children, or parents, in-laws, extended family, friends, and coworkers. Some extended that carrying behavior to their whole world. Women who carry span all categories, from the nurses' aide in your doctor's office to the board member of a Fortune 500 company.

Chapters Three and Four examine the characteristics of these women, focusing on their high expectations of their own performance and a tendency to take control, along with other red flags that signal carrying.

Chapters Five and Six take us through the cycle of carrying—the loop of resolve and resentment that keeps spiraling downward. We also find out about the two-by-four shocks that led these women to reassess their life choices.

Part Two focuses on the changes in these women's lives after they made the deliberate choice to stop carrying. We explore the process of letting loose of control and learning to really listen and hear others. We share the joy and freedom we experienced as we discovered a new definition of loving and a spiritual depth that allowed change to occur.

These women are every woman. They are us. They found solutions. So can we. By making new choices, we can break the cycle of carrying. Making smart choices is worth the effort. It can renew your zest for living and free you to love and live fully. Smart women, smart choices. That's the subject of this book. And we are going to explore those smart choices.

Women and Choice Survey

Before you meet the seven women in the next chapter, let's explore more about your own story. In my work, I have been asking hundreds of women to answer the following ten questions. Take a minute now to write your answers to the questions on a piece of paper. Keep it handy, because in later chapters we will share the results of the survey and you'll have the opportunity to explore your responses. You might find, just as many of us have, that your answers indicate that you, too, are a woman who carries.

Women and Choice Survey

Quickly complete each sentence by writing the first response that comes to mind.

1. I expect others to:

2. I expect myself to:

3. I take control when:

4. I'll take care of:

5. I don't take care of:

6. I need:

7. I don't need:

8. I enjoy receiving:

9. I find encouragement from:

10. I have no choice about:

Chapter 2

Meet Seven Other Smart Women

Reba: The Achiever

Reba, 55, is a successful entrepreneur, flamboyant and bursting with energy and good humor. When the tall, Southern blonde enters a room, everyone senses that something is about to happen.

I was raised in South Carolina in a lower-middle-class home. Although we were probably poor by most standards, I didn't really realize it. From my view, everyone was struggling. We were a typical redneck family, going to revival meetings and eking out a living of sorts. Most of the time, there were just three of us at home—my mother, my father, and myself, although my older stepbrother and stepsister visited occasionally.

My father worked for a paycheck, but his greatest love was gambling. My mother was not happily married—but she was determinedly married. Divorce was not an option for her. Her message to me was: Anyone can marry, but I certainly didn't need to do so.

She told me over and over I was the smartest, most capable person ever. This was the 1950s, and I got a mixed message. My mom was saying marriage was optional, but the world was saying, Get married, be a good wife.

For example, I graduated with the grades to qualify as valedictorian of my small-town high school. But the principal gave the title to a boy and named me salutatorian.

"I made straight A's," I thought. "He didn't. How does that work?"

So I went to our high school principal. He told me the guy got extra credit for being captain of the football team. The real reason, I realized later, was that my schoolmate wanted to go to Stanford. He needed a scholarship to afford the tuition. Being valedictorian improved his chances. As a female, no one thought college was that important for me. Even my parents didn't come to my defense. So, I graduated salutatorian. This was, after all, the 1950s. I got the message.

My father was gone a lot. There was a poker game somewhere every night. But when he came home, he ruled the roost. His word was law. Most of the time, my mom was sad and lonely. I wanted desperately to make her happy. She was my strongest support. Even without a car, she would walk back and forth to bring me things I forgot for school, act as room mother, or lead the Girl Scout troop. So, I grew up trying to take care of her and make her happy. I can remember at age twelve pushing my tall frame through a crowd at a parade so my tiny, five-foot-tall mother could see. I did that kind of thing all the time, playing the husband in many ways.

After high school, I went to a small state college fifty miles from home. It was my only scholarship offer. Bored is an understatement for how I felt there. Courses were so easy I could make A's without going to class. After one year, I quit and came home. I began to date a guy working construction. Most of my friends were married or getting married. So, I married this guy. It was predictive of our short, turbulent relationship that we had two statues on the television—my salutatorian award and his wrestling trophy.

But before we split, I was carrying him in many ways. We moved to the Northwest because jobs were scarce in South Carolina at that time and my older stepbrother lived near Seattle. He found my husband a job as a quality-control specialist at a manufacturing company. I made my husband cheat sheets of chemical formulas he was supposed to know and put them in his pocket so he could do a good job and be promoted.

I was very protective of his ego. That was another message I got from the 1950s: Men had fragile egos and women were supposed to protect them. I might be angry, but I would never say anything to impair that very fragile framework.

But the marriage didn't last long anyway. This guy was a bully, and would do things like hold me in a headlock in front of a mirror and force me to say, "I'm stupid" or "I'm ugly." He thought that was funny. Or he would tickle me until I was in tears and begging for mercy. I might have been stupid to marry him, but I wasn't so dumb as to take that behavior for long. Even though we had a special-needs child, Peter, who required medical and therapeutic help, I left my husband after two years.

Taking care of people was a deep-set habit, though. As a single mom, I even carried my best friend financially. I returned to college and was attending school while working. So was my friend Jenny. We each had one child. We lived in the same government-subsidized apartment building. But for all our similarities in circumstance, she was not very responsible. I did my schoolwork *and* hers, so she would pass. I studied for her exams with her, as well as my own. When Jenny lost her job, I made her and her daughter my special charges. We ate peanut-butter-and-jelly sandwiches, and collected bottles at the end of the month to buy one more week's worth of groceries for the kids. Meanwhile, she wasn't job hunting. By this time, the 1960s era of flower children, love-ins, and peace marches had arrived. Jenny was sitting in the apartment making love beads or something. I carried her and our two children until we both graduated.

But my worst case of carrying was my second husband, Nathan. We were married fifteen years. My husband had three children from his first marriage. They chose to live with us. Little wonder, since his first wife was both on drugs and on welfare. I took care of the four kids and all the household matters, but I was also the financial support.

After I graduated, I accepted a good job with a large company, but was very unhappy, particularly with the inefficiency and office politics. My older brother was my mentor.

"Reba," he counseled, "if you dislike this company, you'll hate working at any large company. It's the system, the way they all operate."

But he also told me that small companies didn't pay as much.

"How about the owner?" I asked. "What kind of money does the owner make?"

"If the business is successful, the owner makes good money," he said.

That settled it for me. I would work in a small business, and be the owner. I could see that the computer field was a growing one, and probably had room for newcomers and women. I opted for the computer field on that basis. I was right. I started my own word processing company and it did well. There was multiple-digit growth, and I was soon part of it.

But even though I proved a sharp businesswoman, I didn't mess with our household budget. I was still hanging on to my girlhood attitude of protecting the male ego. Even though I now had my own company, I gave Nathan complete autonomy over our money. After all, he was the man, I reasoned, and men took care of the family finances.

Nathan was a gambler, like my father. Only Nathan didn't play poker. He played the import-export game. West Coast promoters always had a get-rich-quick idea for some product that could be exported or imported. Nathan always believed the next deal would put us in the big time. Taking on debt was necessary in his mind to get there. But he failed to tell me. I didn't even realize my paycheck was covering all the bills. I didn't find out until one deal in which he had invested heavily fell apart. Suddenly, the creditors were calling. I found out our credit cards—and we had more of them than I realized—were charged to their maximum limits. We were mortgaged to the hilt. Even our teenage son's car, bought on a cosigned note with his dad, had been used as collateral for a loan. I can still see our son's crestfallen face as the car he paid for was hauled out of the front driveway.

I was ready to rethink my life, and what I had done to make this mess possible.

Marta: The Juggler

Marta, 34, is an unassuming, outwardly quiet woman of Hispanic descent, short with long, dark hair. Her intelligence and caring are immediately evident as she speaks.

I spent years taking care of business and family without spending one minute on myself. I was just too busy carrying everyone else to have any time left over.

I was the youngest of three children, born to an ethnically mixed couple. My mother was from Monterrey, Mexico. My father, a serviceman, came from the Deep South, Jackson, Mississippi. They met in Albuquerque, close to where my father was stationed. Both of them came from large families, my mother with fourteen brothers and sisters, my father with nine. My mother, however, moved north and was working as a domestic. She was thirty-five years old when she married my dad. He was twenty-nine.

After I was born, we moved to Phoenix, which was experiencing dramatic growth now that air-conditioning was common. Jobs were plentiful for my father, who now operated a construction crane. My mother stayed home to raise us, but also baby-sat neighborhood children. There might be as many as a dozen children at our home on any given day.

For my parents, the epitome of success for my sister, brother, and me was a high school diploma. Both of them had to drop out of school at a young age just to keep their families going.

Even though I was the youngest, I always took charge. I was caring and nurturing with all the children, and very goal-oriented. I always pushed the limits in anything I did, and was always challenging my parents in their way of thinking. For example, I joined the drill squad in high school, even though my parents thought extracurricular events were a waste of time, and that the short skirts the drill squad wore were scandalous. I was not to be held back by "Old World" thinking.

The biggest challenge was getting to the basketball and football games. My mother didn't drive, and my father was often not available to take me. But I just hustled rides from my friends. My motto was: If I want something, I just figure out how to get it.

I went to the local community college for a year after graduation, but was constantly wondering if I should go to work instead. A high school diploma made me a success in my parents' eyes. Their ambitions for me were fulfilled. I was still living at home, so I quit community college and took a job with a large telecommunications firm.

Fifteen years later, I am still with the same firm. I have been amazed at the opportunities I have been given. One reason I've done so well is that I was always willing to work late, and do the work others left undone. I've been allowed over the years to enter arenas reserved for college-educated workers. In fact, I've been encouraged to try new jobs, and, in some cases, even pushed. Now, I hold a management-level position in the human resources department and am occasionally in planning meetings with the CEO and other top officers. I was always rewarded for devoting long hours to work, so it got to be a habit after a while.

Having children put a crimp in how much overtime I could put in. I married Joe thirteen years ago. We have five children, from twelve years to eighteen months old. But, instead of cutting back, I just kept layering on. Joe had his own business, and sometimes put in seven-day weeks, so I took over the entire household management. My life consisted of endless details. Having a career did not relieve me of the strong Hispanic cultural mores that say a woman takes care of her home and children, *personally.*

When I traveled on business, which I did regularly, I laid out the children's clothes for the course of my entire trip. I made meals and froze them, so all my husband had to do was thaw a package. I typed out a schedule for everyone to follow, listing who was doing what at what time, and who was responsible for taking and picking up. I made the calls to set up carpools and insisted everything run in as timely a manner as a Swiss watch.

Then I spent the last evening before leaving town running the washer and dryer, vacuuming, and cleaning the bathrooms. I knew I should have hired a maid, but, in the Hispanic culture, a woman takes care of her own family and home. My mom ran the family. If I asked my dad's permission for something, he would say, "Ask your mother." Thus, as an adult I did all the cooking, cleaning, and shopping.

My weekends weren't any better. I often went to the office early on Saturday mornings to catch up. Then I spent the rest of the day juggling my kids' sports practices and carpools. Have you ever tried to make two soccer games at the same time? I shopped for groceries on the weekends, plus shopped for the children or household items.

Joe and I didn't even try to make a movie or dinner out. Scheduling a baby-sitter was just one more logistical hurdle to cross for me. My parents lived nearby, and they kept the baby during the week. They took care of all the kids when they were too small for preschool while my husband and I worked. I always felt that I had burdened them enough with having to watch one of our babies during the week. So, asking them to take the kids for the weekend, I felt, was too much. Furthermore, and I know this sounds ungrateful, my parents wouldn't take the children to the park, or to a movie, or do anything special with them when they baby-sat. I almost felt as if it was a punishment to my children if Joe and

I were off doing something fun while they were stuck at Grandma's and Grandpa's house watching television all day.

My parents became, in fact, another area of care for me. They still live nearby. They were aging and asked me for help in home maintenance, shopping, making doctor appointments, and other things. I tried, but I was exhausted. Even a simple task like calling a plumber could take two days before I found time between all the activities at my home and at work. Then, I'd feel guilty for not calling sooner.

I couldn't remember the last time my husband and I had a date. I never had time to read, or walk, or have ten minutes for quiet thought. I couldn't even remember the last time I took a bath without interruption. I knew I needed to get off this fast-moving treadmill, but how?

Sarah: The Fixer

Sarah, 44, is an attractive African-American woman who has risen into corporate senior management through her hard work and the creativity she brings to her position.

Carrying is a pattern with me that goes back to childhood. My sister and I shared a bedroom. My side was neat and organized. Her side looked like a Tasmanian devil had just whirled through—piles of dirty clothes, loose papers, random stuff pitched on the bed and floor.

We were like Felix and Oscar of *The Odd Couple.* I was all over her to get organized and clean up. Finally, I would just clean her side myself. And she would let me. If I wanted the whole room clean, I cleaned it.

So, it was natural for me to take that pattern into marriage. Marvin and I were married right out of high school. He was my first love. We probably got married out of lust. We were very "Hubba, hubba, baby" in high school. We couldn't keep our hands off each other. The beginning of our marriage was much the same, but our paths quickly diverged.

The year was 1974. The Vietnam War was in full force. Marvin was drafted shortly after receiving his high school diploma and sent to

'Nam. Not long thereafter, I discovered I was pregnant. We spent our first year of marriage apart—Marvin in a war zone, I living with my parents in Kansas City. By the time Marvin returned from his twelve-month tour, we were like strangers. Marvin was a veteran of one of America's most divisive and bloody wars. I was a mother. Our daughter, Diane, was born two months before Marvin's return.

The Army moved us to California. I went to work, partially because I liked the independence and partially because Marvin constantly complained about how tough life was. His complaining made me feel guilty for not contributing financially. I started baby-sitting in a nursery and took Diane along. My original ideal was to be a full-time homemaker and stay-at-home mom. I envisioned five kids running around our house. But by the age of twenty-two, I was beginning to realize that Marvin didn't want the full financial responsibility. I began to think in terms of how I might earn more.

I found a job as a secretary with the local chamber of commerce in the California city where we were now stationed. I also took college courses. Marvin worked nights as an Army mechanic, and we alternated child care. We seldom saw each other. Meanwhile, I was being promoted, first as coordinator for meetings, then as supervisor.

As things evolved, I was also making all the family decisions. That started in the second year of the marriage. Then I took on the responsibility for making those decisions work. By the time we had been married ten years, I was running the whole show.

Two important events converged in 1977. A young computer company offered me a job in their training department. And the Army wanted Marvin to do a three-year tour of duty in Germany. If the family didn't go with him, the Army would reduce the tour to two years.

"I'm not going," I told him after some long thought. "You make your own decision about what's best for you. We'll be here when you return."

Marvin elected to leave the Army. At that point, I really took the lead. While Marvin was in the Army, our incomes were about equal. My subsequent promotion took us to a new city. Marvin worked as a mechanic, but he wasn't happy.

"I hate this city," he told me, "and I hate the people."

Then a car accident put him in rehabilitation for two years. Meanwhile, I continued to progress at work, eventually becoming a senior vice president. By now, I was the sole breadwinner.

Over the next ten years of our marriage, that would prove our undoing.

But I wasn't just running the home front. My pattern of carrying continued at work. I would let people put the monkey on my back. I'd be at work until nine o'clock or ten o'clock at night, even though others had left promptly at five to be with their families.

My reaction to our merger with another company was a prime example of my modus operandi. I was already spending most of my waking hours on the job. Our company acquired a competitor of about equal size. It was the biggest step we ever took in terms of stretching and growing. Senior management told me, "Okay, within six months we've got to integrate twenty-five hundred people into our culture. Your department needs to take on most of that responsibility." My ten-hour days turned into fourteen-hour days.

So, did I delegate? People were asking me, "Can I help? Can I help?" And I answered with "Later," or "I'll get back to you."

It was a perfect opportunity to bring in lots of people. It was a new situation for all of us. We were learning as we went.

But I was doing it by myself, unable to let loose. I was flying between two states, putting in one long day after another, going through all this emotional stuff with different employee groups, explaining the coming transformation, setting up everything.

I went into my really focused mode. I was too busy organizing in my head to explain the big picture to a lot of people. I had a couple of coworkers who were close to me, and understood what I was going through. But that's it.

Finally, those who wanted to help quit asking if they could. I guess they figured (correctly) that I was going to do it all myself. By the time the six months were up, I was close to a breakdown, suffering complete exhaustion.

Michelle: The Mother Hen

Michelle, 39, is a courageous African-American woman who lights up a room with her smile.

At twenty, I lost both my kidneys. That was in 1978. Except for a brief period in the 1980s when I had a kidney transplant that ultimately failed, I have had to hook up to a dialysis machine six hours a night, three times a week, to clean my blood. But being disabled never stopped me from carrying the financial load for my husband and myself, or from taking on another's work at my job. It was just in my system, I guess.

My mom and dad were divorced. My mom remarried and had two more children. When she returned to work, I took care of them after school. I was in junior high and they were in first and second grades. I didn't mind. I loved my brother and sister. I was like the mother hen, making sure they did their homework, feeding them, bathing them at night. Mom worked the late shift and didn't get home until 11 P.M. I would still be up then trying to finish my own schoolwork.

Even on holidays, I made the festivities happen: the birthday cake, the Easter eggs, and the Christmas cookies. I walked to the five-and-dime and bought crepe paper and hung streamers over the kitchen table every time someone had a birthday.

I loved those babies. I couldn't even get mad when they bothered my dates in high school, hiding behind the couch or spying on us from the kitchen. I pretty much raised them until I left for college.

I was popular in high school. I was little and cute and had several guys asking me out up until I developed kidney problems and became very ill. At one point, I even lost my eyesight, but, by the grace of God, I believe, and through the prayers of my church family, my eyesight was restored. My life centered around church and school in the small town where I was raised. My mother and grandmother were strong role models. They taught me to pray, to respect my elders, and to be responsible.

I fell passionately in love while I was in college with a guy I knew from my hometown. He joined the service after high school, but we wrote letters and saw each other occasionally. I tasted passion with him.

When I became ill again and finally lost my kidneys, I lost my boyfriend at the same time. He was stationed in Germany when I last heard from him. There was no official breakup. We simply stopped writing. I guess we both understood that he couldn't deal with a woman who was permanently hooked up to a dialysis machine.

I finished an associate's degree and started to work at a state agency as a secretary. I moved away from my family because only a large city gave me access to dialysis. My mom helped me move and for many years, she was my chief support system, coming to visit once a month and making sure I had what I needed.

I became the mother hen at work, too. The men would come and tell me their problems. "Michelle, I need to talk with you," they would say. And they would pour out their difficulties, whether it was about their marriages, children, or finances. "What do you think?" they would ask. I enjoyed it. I got to be the mom again, sympathizing, offering advice, holding someone's hand.

From there I became the office party giver. Every time someone had a birthday, I baked the cake. I also became the person who tracked supplies, making sure we had everything we needed, right down to toilet paper.

It was just a short step from there to helping out everyone on their workload. By now, I knew how to do everything. The men would let me finish their reports, track down a missing order, straighten out a customer complaint. I was even doing the screening on job applicants. None of this was in my job description, just my soul.

Meanwhile, I had blocked out the thought of ever having a boyfriend. I did carry the memory of the passion from my first boyfriend with me, but I was confident I would never experience that kind of romantic love again. Dialysis changes your appearance. I was rail-thin and weak. My hair fell out. My skin turned dark and ashen—it looked like tar.

Then I met Lionel at church. "How are you doing, Miss Lady," he said. I was thrilled to have a handsome, sophisticated man call me "Miss Lady." He made me feel pretty again.

We began to go out with a group, and Lionel was always very tender with me. He was the lead singer in a local band and had lots of lady friends. I knew that, but I was pleased to be his friend. As a work- and church-centered girl, it was an adventure for me to go to the clubs with him. And I felt safe with Lionel. He always looked out for me.

Lionel began to ask me why I always wore long sleeves and wigs, so I told him about the dialysis. I wore long sleeves to cover up the bandaged bumps caused by the needles that pierced my skin three times a week. I wore wigs to cover up my short, stubby hair caused by dialysis.

"So what," he said. "You're a good-looking woman. A few bandages don't matter."

I began to wear shorter skirts and short-sleeved blouses. He got me to quit wearing wigs. Instead, I styled my short locks in a bob close to my head. It looked almost stylish, in an avant-garde way. He encouraged me to grow my nails long, which I did. I polished them to a fine shine with bright nail polish. I began to feel pretty. I loved all the attention.

My worldly and street-wise friend, Lionel, also dated other women. But, over time, we became more than friends. We became lovers. Lionel reawakened the sexual urge I had lost.

When he proposed marriage, I said no. I told him he didn't understand my life, really. The dialysis machine was not a pretty picture. So he spent nights with me while I went through treatments and drove me home afterwards. I made sure he understood about dialysis. I told him I would always be sick, off and on. I might lose my job because of my disability. I couldn't have children. I couldn't imagine any man wanting to marry a woman who couldn't have children. It was my biggest heartache. I loved children so much.

Still, he stayed. By now we were living together, an arrangement my mother was very much against. But I needed someone and I loved him so much.

I was always taught marriage is forever, and didn't want to chance a divorce. I told Lionel that if he wanted someone else, I would step aside. I was used to being put aside by then. I felt I could always go back to my world of church, work, and home. Then finally, I took the big step and told him I wanted to get married.

Lionel told me he had to clean up some relationships before he could commit to me. He never lied about that.

When we married, we moved into my apartment. I had the stuff—furniture, television, stereo, dishes. Lionel was a musician and worked construction when he needed money. But after a while, he quit the construction. By the time we'd been married for three years, I was pretty much the financial support. The money from his gigs went into his pocket, not to pay our bills. But the stress of carrying all the financial responsibility was hurting my health. Dialysis makes you fight for life, and it is a tough fight. Additional stresses can pull you down pretty quickly. I went through a period of needing extra blood transfusions, three or four a month, and I couldn't go on.

I quit my job, even though I had moved from being a secretary to an administrative position. I was making good money. I even had my own secretary. I was paid once a month, but by the time I paid all the bills, I was broke again. And then Lionel would come home with an attitude, like maybe he was going to give me spending money this week, or maybe he wasn't. That's all he did—provide spending money. So, I turned in my two weeks' notice and quit my job.

I quit carrying Lionel. I told him it was up to him. It really tripped him out. He didn't know what to do. But he came through. He got a factory job and he managed to make the house payments and the car payment. Sometimes he had to ask for an advance on his paycheck, but he managed. I went back to school and upgraded my computer skills.

I didn't go back to work for two years. But when I did, we fell back into the old pattern again. Lionel went back to playing in clubs. I became the chief breadwinner, paying all the bills.

However, the next crisis would really stretch our ability to survive as husband and wife. And my dialysis became harder and harder to bear. I wasn't going to be able to carry forever.

Tamara: The Doer

Tamara, 45, is a beautiful, athletic artist of Irish descent. She meets life with an untiring grace somewhere between the Energizer bunny's and a saint's.

Phil and I are happily married. But our success is the result of many changes on both our parts. Together, we had to learn through crisis how to forge a successful relationship. It hasn't been easy. "Marriage is like farming," Phil now says. "Every day you get up and start all over again."

I was devastated when my first husband left me and our three small children. Raised in the Catholic church, I never let divorce enter my thoughts. Jack was a disinterested father and husband. We seldom talked. Still, I thought marriage was a lifetime commitment.

After Jack left, I pulled myself together, found a job at an insurance agency, sold the home I could not afford to maintain on my own, moved into an apartment, and got on with life. My motto became: "I can do this."

One day I was jogging at the high school track next door to where the children were in child care. Phil jogged up beside me. I talked to Phil but turned him down when he asked me out. I wasn't interested.

A year later, Phil saw my daughter at the high school and recognized Susie as my child by her eyes. "You are Tamara's daughter?" he asked. Getting an affirmative answer, he found me coaching my son's basketball team in the gym. This time, he invited me to a reading from his recently completed play. Curious, I went.

It was his creative writing that touched my heart. Coming from my first marriage to a man who couldn't express a single feeling, it was very important to me to find a man who could. I wanted a man who could *own* his feelings.

We started to date. We both recognized immediately that something spiritual and higher than the two of us was happening. We spent hours reading the Bible on dates, something I had never done in my life, much less with a man. We talked often about the fact that there was some other purpose in our coming together. We were just instruments.

I also knew Phil was not a good candidate for a support system for me and the kids. He had a history of job-hopping. We married anyway.

The honeymoon didn't last long. Within a week after the wedding, Phil was fired from his position as a tennis coach. He had owned businesses before—a small advertising agency and an auto parts store. Now, he encouraged me to go to a commercial art institute to develop my natural artistic talents. He, in turn, would start another advertising agency. The idea appealed to me.

I really went out on a limb. I shifted to part time at the insurance company to bring in an income and used the savings from the sale of my home to make up the difference in pay from full-time to half-time work. I did this for three years while I attended school. What I had most was the inspiration of hope. I needed it.

I soon found myself living a tough schedule. Up at 5 A.M., going to work in the mornings and to art school in the afternoon, and returning home to care for the children in the early evening. Late in the evening, I would start my homework, plus do advertising layouts for Phil's new business. Bedtime didn't come until after midnight.

To complicate matters, Phil's mother asked to live with us. She was nearly destitute, and we had just rented a nice home with four bedrooms. We had the space. How could we say no? But Phil's mom was an alcoholic. Her frequent bouts of depression and anger caused emotional upheavals among all of us—Phil, myself, the children. Within the year, we realized this arrangement was not going to work. Phil talked his aunt into taking his mother in.

But I persevered. I had a strong need to be loved. I needed someone there. I had a lot of responsibility growing up, and I felt needed, but not loved. My father, a salesman, was absent a lot. Mom had the job of child-rearing. She was a good worker, but her self-esteem wasn't good. She always felt inferior to her own sisters, the neighbors, the women at church. She approached motherhood as a job to be done. She didn't show love in demonstrative ways. I was the same way. I worked to get done whatever needed to be done without complaint because of the unspoken fear that, if I expected more, my husband might leave.

Within two years, life began to improve for a short time. I graduated and went to work full time in our advertising business. Phil, dynamic and personable, made friends easily. He was invited to join several nonprofit boards, gaining a foothold in the community and bringing in business. But over the next four years, everything disintegrated.

Phil was unhappy. He really wanted to devote his time to creative writing. He began to sleep late, not showing up at the office until 11 A.M., then going to lunch and playing tennis in the afternoon. I began to resent the fact that I was at the office early and doing most of the work.

Then, Phil disappeared from the business altogether—watching movies at night and sleeping during the day. He was supposed to be handling the family budget. But, as creditors began to call, I realized nothing was being paid. House payments were behind, the office rent was in arrears, other bills were overdue.

I was really angry and found it hard to talk to him. When I did try to talk with Phil, he would get angry and yell. So I shut down emotionally from him.

Then came an important insight. I realized I couldn't change him . . . or anybody, for that matter. A feeling of total hopelessness set in. On that realization, I made some decisions. I separated myself from the advertising agency and started my own graphic-design firm. Phil and the agency ended up in bankruptcy court. And I left him. Our home was repossessed, and I moved myself and the children into a small rented house and worked from there. Phil called, but I had nothing to say. He threw away what we had built. I was too hurt and too angry to talk.

It took a Christmas miracle to bring us back together.

Joan: The Determined One

Joan, 51, is a slim redhead from the Northeast with a commanding presence and a tender heart.

Remember Lucy from the *Peanuts* comic strip? Miss know-it-all, bossy, I'm-always-right Lucy? That was me with my older sister and younger brother growing up. I was the middle child, but the dominant personality. I generally picked the games we played and decided who would play which role in our favorite pastime of let's pretend.

I loved to read, and I was smart. School was a no-brainer. Decent grades came easily.

But there was another side. The I'll-never-be-as-pretty-as-my-mother-or-as-smart-as-my-daddy side. My father was a successful, self-made businessman. My mother was Mrs. Charity Ball. My sister, brother, and I had every advantage. Private schools, lessons in everything from how to sit a horse to how to play music to which fork to use at a formal dinner. Our parents wanted us to be perfect. The only time my mother spanked me was when I embarrassed her by misbehaving in public. Otherwise, discipline was lax at our house. So, while I was in control within the home, I was timid and scared outside of it. I knew I was not perfect, regardless of the facade I so gamely put forth.

My parents' plans for me went awry with the Vietnam War. My sympathies lay with the flower children who were chanting, "Make love, not war." My parents saw only the danger of sedition and drugs. The nation and my family erupted into generational warfare.

I was totally confused, and so naive from a protected childhood that I didn't recognize danger. I married a man who was domineering and abusive. My father was gentle and loving. I didn't even know men *could* be abusive. I found out. The first year he threw me on the ground and with a contorted grimace raised his fist to smash my face. He didn't, but I got the message. Scared of his temper, I dutifully let him lead to keep peace. Eight years and two kids later, I was a shrinking violet with little of my original Lucy left.

In the midst of a deep depression, I got an angel message. "Do not be afraid. The answers will come," I was told. My visitant enveloped me in a love I had long missed, and I knew that my parents were right. I was the loved child of God. The depression ended. Lucy rose from the ashes. I refused to be a doormat to my husband's wishes any longer. I began to treat him as he treated me. I thought he would see how awful his behavior was and change. I was wrong. The violence increased as I took an aggressive stand. But I stood firm. My husband must have scared himself, because one day, six weeks after my spiritual experience, he came home and announced he was moving out.

For the next seven years, I was a single mom. During that time, I went back to school, earned a second degree, went to work, and did well in my chosen profession. I became very independent.

When I later married Allen I knew I would continue to carry the main load financially. I had established a good career as a public-relations specialist in a major city. Now, at the age of thirty-six, I was comfortable that I could support my family.

But finding someone to fill the gap left by divorce was not proving easy. When Allen came along, I found a companion in a sweet man who shared my love of family and home. Allen didn't earn much money, barely enough for a single man. Certainly not enough to support a family, particularly with the expectations I had for my own family. But his innate character was wonderful. He was so innocent and so pure. I loved those qualities. I can support myself and my children, I thought.

I knew my ambitions and goals for our family were greater than Allen's. He was younger, had never been married, and, I felt, did not realize how much money it took to support a family. From the first day of our marriage, I took the lead. I accepted a job in another city that moved me into a management position and doubled my income. Allen followed, but over the course of several years, never found comparable employment.

Early in our new marriage, we had a baby, a third child for me, a first for Allen. We called her Angela. Allen adored his small daughter. There was never any doubt in either of our minds that we belonged together as a family.

But my initial intention to be the main breadwinner was proving harder than I had envisioned. Although I was by now head of public relations at a large advertising agency, I felt pressure to earn even more money with our older children approaching college age. In fact, I felt I had to provide a monetary trust for my children as my father had done for me. I started my own public-relations company, thinking this was the way to build wealth. It proved to be hard. Shortly after starting the company, the bottom fell out of the economy. Companies were failing in the depressed market. We held on, but only by my working longer and longer hours.

I took the same attitude at work as I had at home. It was all on my shoulders. I had to come up with solutions. As boss, I felt I had to set an example. But I did more than that. I was doing everything. When the secretary complained about not having enough time to finish stuffing the mailing envelopes, I stayed late and helped her. We were there until 10 P.M. When the account executive said he didn't have time to call on all the clients, I took over some of the calls myself. When the production coordinator was in a bind, I stayed to proofread or do "whatever it takes." I was carrying half the office, in addition to my own administrative, management, and planning responsibilities.

We forged an alliance with a bigger agency to infuse money into the company and expand its capabilities into the national advertising arena. Unfortunately, the agency was bought out, and the deal fell through. After seven years of intensely hard work, I was exhausted. I sold the company on a future promise of money if the new owner did well. Then I went home, too tired even to think of job hunting.

After the sale, Allen, who by this time had joined the company to help in the proposed expansion, was jobless, too.

"It's up to you," I told him. I was too tired to carry the load further. My initial intention to carry the family financially was proving too tough.

Kate: The Adviser

Kate, 37, is a large-boned woman of Native American heritage. Extremely smart and analytical, there is another side to Kate that draws people to her side "just to quietly talk and share."

I grew up with two passions—learning and helping. While these have turned out to be my greatest assets in life, in the beginning they were my nemesis. It was these characteristics that led me to carry.

My dad was in sales and we moved almost yearly. Not a problem. I was quickly able to make new friends. And I was smart. So I was able to keep up with my studies and perform at the top of my class no matter where I lived. My classmates soon learned they could come to me for help with anything they needed—from assistance with homework to an ear for their problems with parents or friends.

The same pattern followed me into my marriage. Richard and I were high school sweethearts. He was not very emotionally demanding, and it was a relief to spend time with him having fun. I was a junior in college and Richard a senior when we married. We worked for a year and then returned to school, I working full time and going to school part time, Richard working part time and finishing school on a full-time basis.

Most of the nine years Richard and I were married he was, well, missing in action. I should have recognized a red flag when he showed up at our wedding without the ring. Richard was just not there, emotionally or physically. From day one, he abdicated responsibility to me.

I knew from our dating days that he was not financially responsible. He would bounce checks frequently, not because he didn't know how to balance a checkbook, but because he didn't take the time to attend to it. So I took over the household budget right after we were married, and Richard was glad to hand over the job.

After graduation he earned a good living as a CPA, but he did not take care of other responsibilities. Over the years, one by one, I found myself making all the decisions and managing the entire household without Richard's input. The weight of the load grew with time, and, with each new crisis, became heavier and heavier. It also seemed that as he passed off each responsibility, he pulled further away emotionally. So during the tough times, he wasn't there for me. And tough times came.

One stress was the years of infertility. Emotionally, Richard took his infertility personally and withdrew even further from me. Eventually, we ended up going to an infertility specialist and saw a marriage counselor. During that time, we made some progress and I became pregnant. Our only daughter, a miracle baby, brought us closer for a short time.

Then, I was in an automobile accident and Richard had to take over most of the household responsibilities for a few months. He took our baby, Joy, to day care and took over most of the parental duties at night. But it proved to be too much for Richard and things just didn't get done. As soon as I was back on my feet, I again plunged into taking on more and more of the responsibility for maintaining our home. But by then, I was on maximum overload as I continued to take on more responsibility at work, also.

During my married years, I worked in many different industries—from banking and insurance to high tech and real estate. I loved the challenge of doing so many different things and, as it turned out, it equipped me with a unique store of knowledge. Regardless of what position I held, I was always the one who saw the bigger picture, because I would learn my job and the job of everyone around me. I became a focal point of information in the organization, which made me in high demand. Before long, my coworkers were looking to me to explain or, better yet, to complete various projects for them. I had very high standards, and was happy to oblige so that the job would be done to my level of quality. Coworkers also found it easy to talk to me about their personal problems, and what little time I had to spare disappeared. It proved to be too much. The carrying I was doing, combined with the inefficiency of large corporations in general, grated against my perfectionist standards.

Despite my success, I was miserable in corporate America. So I started a printing company on the side and worked both jobs for about a year, with the intention of going out totally on my own. Business was good, so I decided I could quit my corporate job. I told Richard of my decision. But his surprise for me was even bigger. He announced he was moving out.

What little safety net I had dropped away. We had been on parallel paths, and we hadn't connected emotionally in a long time. But I couldn't return to work in corporate America. I was too burned out. What to do next . . . ?

After the divorce, I took a new path. With a newfound faith, I sold my printing company, started a consulting business, and enrolled in graduate school. I realized I could support our daughter and survive without Richard.

But my carrying didn't end with my divorce. After my mother and father divorced, my mother began to lean on me even more. After all, she hadn't worked for years and needed a job. She didn't know where to start, I reasoned. And she had to sell the house and move. And then there were all the legal papers . . . Lucky that I knew a lot about all that and could help, although it loaded even more on my plate. And along with her came the problems of her three widowed, elderly sisters who needed help with Medicare forms and car insurance and health problems. But I loved them, and knew I had knowledge that would help, so I willingly took on the job of chief family adviser and rescuer.

It would be some time yet before I realized how carrying others was leading me—and them—into a deep abyss.

These seven women also completed the Women and Choice Survey in Chapter One. Their answers were similar to the responses of hundreds of other high-achieving women that I surveyed. These answers, shown on the next page, give us insight into how they think and operate in their worlds—their expectations of themselves and others, their priorities, their needs, their wants, their choices.

In the next chapter, we'll explore the expectations of women who carry and how those expectations lead them to crossing the line to carrying.

Women and Choice Survey Results

The results below represent the most common answers given by the hundreds of women surveyed, and the percentage of the group that gave each response.

1. *I expect others to:*
Do what they say they will	20%
Be respectful of me and others	20%
Be kind and considerate	19%

2. *I expect myself to:*
Do my best/be perfect	22%
Succeed/excel	13%

3. *I take control when:*
I feel it's necessary	34%
No one else does	17%

4. *I'll take care of:*
My family	26%
Myself	19%
Everything	17%

5. *I don't take care of:*
Me	40%
Housework	13%

6. *I need:*
Love/support	26%
Time for self	17%

7. *I don't need:*
Negativity	22%
Money/status	10%

8. *I enjoy receiving:*
Praise/recognition	39%
Flowers/gifts/money	20%
Love/support/encouragement	16%

9. *I find encouragement from:*
Friends/coworkers	25%
Family	18%
Doing a good job	11%

10. *I have no choice about:*
What others choose	13%
My family	7%
I always have a choice	7%

Your Story

How do your answers compare to theirs?

Similarities:

Differences:

Chapter 3
Expectations That Lead to Carrying

Smart women have high expectations of themselves and what they should be accomplishing. We often don't know the difference between getting something done and getting something done well. We feel it *must* be done well.

If others are involved in the task, we hold them to our standards and methods. In other words, we take control. These lesser mortals (in our minds) are often quite tickled to give us the control, as long as we also do the work.

"Do you understand how to make the report more readable using tables and boxes?"

"No, they didn't teach us that in our class on Word 6.0."

"Never mind. Give it to me as is, and I'll finish it."

"Okay." (Look of relief.)

High expectations set the stage for carrying. When others don't meet our expectations, we just pick them up and carry them along. After all, we have schedules to meet, projects with deadlines, a home to manage. Some of us even schedule our lovemaking, looking at our calendars and figuring out when we can take time for romance.

"Okay, dear, my calendar is open a week from Saturday for a quiet dinner, just the two of us."

Kind of takes the spontaneity out of sex, doesn't it?

Of course, we never demand more of others than we demand of ourselves. And we don't need anyone else to nag us about *our* responsibilities because we expect so much from ourselves. We believe we *should* be able to do it all. We believe we *should* be able to handle everything. We believe we *should* know the answers. After all, we are smart women.

Of course, we find ourselves overcommitted. Still, even when we realize we've taken on too much, we are willing to do almost anything to keep the ball rolling, even if it means not seeing our family for days, or surviving on two hours of sleep a night. Our worst nightmare is dropping the ball.

Invariably, that ball does drop, however. We get sick, or burn out, or an emergency interrupts our script for the game. When we do drop the ball, rather than just "fessing up," as my mother would phrase it, we become defensive and feel guilty. More than anyone else, we have let ourselves down, because we believe we should always meet our goals.

Our Expectations of Ourselves

I-can-do-it Attitude

Among my friends, these high expectations of self developed at different times in their lives. For some, the expectations started at an early age, often encouraged by parents. For others, our expectations grew as we reached adulthood and began to realize our capabilities in the working world. Some appear to have an internal drive that pushes them on to excellence, regardless of their surroundings. But all of them have an "I-can-do-it" attitude. Reba, Joan, and Tamara represent this spectrum of self-expectation by achieving women.

Reba: Grade-school entrepreneur

I always felt that I could do anything I wanted. As an adult, I can see the large role my mother played in generating that sense of confidence and high expectation.

She was incredibly supportive. My very earliest memories are of her telling me how smart, and pretty, and capable I was. I never doubted her. But, from the perspective of an adult, I can also see how she protected me, achieving in her own way her own standard of excellence for "sheltering" motherhood.

My gambling father's idea of the good life was living in a hotel and driving a big car with a big cigar in his mouth. My mom wanted a home. She scraped together enough to put a down payment on a duplex. I guess she figured she'd earn enough from the rent on half the house to make the monthly payment.

But at one point, my father must have run up some big debts, because my mom had to rent out both halves of the house to make ends meet. I don't know where Dad was, but she and I had to move into the chicken coop at the back of the house. We lived there all summer. She strung a lightbulb from an extension cord and moved an old wood-burning stove into the coop. The floor was dirt. I can still see her sweeping that dirt floor.

But she didn't let on to me that life was hard. I was still little, and she made the summer into a great adventure. She sang to me, we played games, and laughed. She popped popcorn on the stove. My little neighborhood friend was envious, and wanted to move in and "camp out" with us. I never realized until much later that it must have been a tough time for my mother.

So, it wasn't just a case of her telling me I was smart and capable. It was also the day-to-day example she set of how much a woman could accomplish. I might come home from school and find she had single-handedly knocked out a wall and was building a floor-to-ceiling bookshelf. We would go window shopping, and I would point out the clothes I liked. Then, we would go home and she would make them for me. She could put together a dress in an afternoon. She was a doer.

I was a doer, too. Even as a kindergartner, I took my mother's empty perfume bottles, filled them with water, and sold them to the neighborhood ladies. To earn money in elementary school, I would sell entertainment. No one had air-conditioning, and everyone was on their front porches at night. I would tell a story for a nickel. For fifty cents, I would sing and dance. At the end of the summer, I would organize a circus with the other children, and sell tickets. By the time I got to high school, I blew off baby-sitting at 25 cents an hour. All the girls baby-sat, but I found out some of the guys were being paid one dollar an hour to drive a tractor out in the country.

"I can do that," I thought.

So I got a job driving a tractor and hauling hay. In high school, I also tutored Latin.

I really had a "can-do" attitude. When my friends had problems, they asked me for solutions. I always had one. It never occurred to me that I might not. So, by the time I got to college, my expectations for myself were very high indeed. I figured I could do anything I wanted.

So I decided to do everything. I just kept layering on to my responsibilities. I took a full course load. I worked full time at a department store in town, and tutored languages at night. I typed other people's reports for money. My older stepbrother was having financial difficulties, so I sent him money every month. I sent money to my mother. I joined the French Society, and within a year, I was running it, painting recruiting posters at 2 A.M.

Later, after marriage and divorce, I supported myself, my friend Jenny, and our two children, and kept a full course load each semester. I wasn't to be stopped.

Tamara: Sleep is for sissies

I approached life from the standpoint that you did what had to be done, even if that meant picking up the slack from others who weren't pulling their weight. From the beginning of that philosophy, I got an increasing amount done from day to day and year to year. My expectations and my standards grew as I proved my ability to myself.

By the time I remarried in my early thirties, I was amazed at just how much had to be done. But I did it. My philosophy didn't change. My favorite T-shirt said, "Sleep is for sissies."

A typical day for me after Phil and I were married went something like this: up at 5 A.M., dress, grab a cup of coffee, lay out the kids' clothes for school, make their lunches and mine (I also took a brown-bag lunch everyday, because of our limited budget) and be at the bus stop by 6 A.M. The bus ride to downtown was an hour and a half from our outlying town. If I was lucky, and the bus wasn't too crowded or noisy, I caught a few more winks on the way.

By 8 A.M. I was at my desk. At noon, I clocked out and rode the bus to the art institute where I was taking classes for a degree in commercial art. I ate my lunch in the park area outside the institute and attended classes until 4 P.M. Then I caught the bus again, arriving home around 6 P.M.

Once home, it was time to check in with the kids and Phil, make dinner and help with homework, run a load of wash, go to the grocery store, or whatever seemed the top priority to keep us all going. Around 10 P.M., the children would be in bed, and I would start my homework. Many nights I also did advertising layouts for Phil's business. I seldom made it to bed before 1 A.M.

Looking back on it, I guess I really did have high expectations for myself, although I didn't really realize it at the time. I was just doing what had to be done, even when it meant taking on more and more responsibilities. That's what got me in trouble.

Joan: The great pretender

My early expectations of myself came through my family. People were constantly referring to my father with awe in their voices. He was a self-made man, a super high achiever who made Eagle Scout even when there was no scout troop in his small town, who had been engineering plants and overseeing a staff of hundreds in his mid-twenties. My mom was really smart, too. I can remember the year she was president of three clubs and never missed putting a meal on the table.

My parents emphasized education. They were both college educated, my father with a master's degree. My mom would rave about my cousin who made straight A's. Two of my cousins got full scholarships to Ivy League colleges. My mom would tell me I was perfect and I could do anything. Only I didn't really feel perfect. I felt more like I was *pretending* to be perfect. So, I made good grades, but not great grades. I joined clubs, and served as an officer. I did what was expected of me . . . to a point.

I figured that all women born into my family would just automatically be upper-middle class, as if you could be born into the Junior League. It never even occurred to me that you had to go out and work. That sounds stupid, but it was a reasonable assumption, given my background. When I married, I didn't have a clear sense of personal direction. But I did come from a very loving family. And I kept the peace in my marriage through love. I let my controlling husband have his way. But in that peacekeeping mission, I lost myself.

After our divorce, I didn't have a clue how I would support myself and my children. My father took an incredibly strong stand at that low point in my life. He sat at my kitchen table. Tears were rolling down his cheeks. I had only seen my father cry twice. This was one of those times, so I knew what he did was tough, and out of love. He said, "If I help you financially, I won't be helping you. You have to do this alone."

And I did. In that process, I realized, Hey, I really am very capable. Then I began to achieve *my* dreams, not someone else's. I began to march to my own drummer, and my expectations of myself grew. I did well at work, and was promoted, and promoted, and promoted. Other companies recruited me.

I still carried some childhood expectations into this newfound confidence, however. I felt I must build wealth. My father had, and since I had taken on the task of chief breadwinner, building wealth was part of my expectation of what a breadwinner does. Just supporting my family wasn't enough. Through my father, I had a small trust fund. It provided for a few extras, and I was very grateful to have it. I thought I must create enough wealth to set up a trust fund for my children, a source of secondary income.

I didn't expect Allen to support us when he and I were married. He was loving and sweet, and he didn't expect me to change to fit his idea of a wife. That was so appealing to me after my first marriage. Being the chief financial support in this marriage was a very, very deliberate decision on my part. All I asked was for Allen to support himself.

After our daughter Angela was born, however, I did expect Allen to become serious about earning more money. Based on my background, my idea of what it took financially to raise a family was high. I thought you had to live in a nice house in a nice neighborhood with good schools. I thought you had to send your kids to camp. I thought you had to give them music lessons. I thought you had to dress them nicely and take them on family vacations.

I thought Allen would be more aggressive about earning a living. But his expectations and mine didn't match. So, the pressure stayed on me to build the family stake.

Always Meet Commitments

You have probably heard the old truism "If you want something done, give it to a busy person." We choose the most reliable person we can find to do the job. And reliable people don't quit until the job is done. The

PTA president will be up at 2 A.M. writing thank-you notes to the mothers who helped give the teacher-appreciation luncheon. That's exactly why *she* is president, and not the woman who will tell you later that she meant to write those notes but "just got too busy."

Those of us who carry expect ourselves to complete all things we commit to do, regardless of what it takes. Commitment also has much to do with why we keep taking on more responsibilities. We are committed to doing our best, and often, to get the job done right, we think we have to do it ourselves. It's our commitment that keeps us working after everyone else has gone home, or that keeps us serving on too many committees.

Commitment can be a positive force. Certainly, no relationship, even the best one in which equal partners are working toward a common goal, can exist for long without commitment. Commitment, along with perseverance, gets us through the rough spots. But sometimes commitment becomes an obstacle to positive change.

Sarah: The elixir of work

Work was my elixir. I got all my strokes from work. As a high school graduate with ambitions of raising a house full of kids, I had risen further up the corporate ladder than I ever could have dreamed. I had gone from an entry-level position to senior vice president over the course of twenty years.

Home was a different story. From the time our daughter, Diane, was little, my husband and I fought over how to raise her. Marvin was a "because I said so" type of parent. He was very conservative, and really wanted to keep a tight rein. I wanted to give her as much choice and freedom as possible at every stage of development. By the time our daughter was two years old, I had decided it wouldn't be fair or right to have another, considering how differently Marvin and I approached child-rearing. So I poured myself into work.

Work was going well. It was not uncommon once Diane was in

high school for me to stay at the office until 10 P.M. There was never any shortage of work to do. I felt very grateful to the management of this company for giving me so many chances and allowing me to grow with it. I was totally committed. I had a real need to feel significant, and work filled that need.

Michelle: Make it work

I was carrying my husband, making decisions about our life together, keeping the finances, and earning most of our living out of a sense of obligation. This goes way back to my childhood expectations. I was determined that when I got married, I was going to make it work. My parents were divorced when I was little, and I just decided that I was never going to give up on my relationship. That set the stage for never knowing when to say enough is enough. When I committed to something, I set my mind to it and did it. So, more than from just wanting to help Lionel, my actions came from a sense of commitment to the relationship. In my mind, I made every effort toward making that work. I was committed to the *idea* of a relationship, rather than *this* relationship. The commitment was not because of Lionel. It was because of my giving, committed nature. And that's a gift, unless it goes too far.

Low-Maintenance Women

I always considered myself to be a "low-maintenance" woman, an independent soul who needed very little in the way of nurturing or reassurance.

As I said to my husband shortly after our marriage, "You told me you loved me when we got married. If anything changes, let me know."

Otherwise, I didn't expect him to say "I love you" every day. I really didn't. Life was to be gotten on with. And I was ready to go.

We are women who need no help from others, and we don't have time to care for ourselves. So we ignore our own needs, or, worse, never even recognize that we have needs.

Women who carry juggle so many tasks that we leave no room for taking care of ourselves. Have you ever brushed your teeth, mouth foaming, and made your bed simultaneously? I have. Have you ever sat in a business meeting while writing down notes for a proposal you plan to write later that day? I have. Have you ever cooked dinner while talking on the phone to a client and gesticulating wildly to your child about sitting down and starting his homework? Tamara's story is typical.

Tamara: The pencil-strategy lunch

When I worked at the insurance company, I spent my lunch hours running errands. It was easier to do at lunch because I didn't have my children in tow. Even after I was self-employed, I often used lunchtime, when my clients were unlikely to call, to run errands. I called it the "pencil-strategy lunch." I would pencil a list of everything that needed to be done, then decide how much I could accomplish by carefully planning my stops, making sure the route was as efficient as possible. For example, I would pick up pantyhose at the department store and, since I was there, I would go by the toy department to get a gift for a birthday party one of the children had been invited to on Saturday. I tried to do as much one-stop shopping as possible. On the way back, I might stop to drop off some film. I was obsessed with how much I could get done at lunchtime. If I ate lunch at all, it was usually out of my lap in the car or at my desk.

Nights were for taking care of family. So were weekends. It's true what they say about mothers not being able to get sick. When I'm in the bathroom throwing up, some kid is yelling, "Mom, where are my shoes?" My husband is yelling, "Have you seen my keys?" And, true to form, I struggle to my feet and find the missing items.

Sarah: No rose for me

One dreary day in February we had an emergency in my department. Everyone pitched in, stayed late, and fixed a potentially harmful mistake.

The next morning I called the florist to order a rose delivered to each person in appreciation for their work. The roses were delivered to the men as well as the women. The staff responded so positively, particularly the men. For many of them, it was their first rose. The only person who didn't get a thank-you flower was me. It never occurred to me to order a rose for myself. I should have done so. It would have made me feel good, too.

Marta: Just tennis shoes

One Christmas all I asked my husband for was a pair of tennis shoes. Granted, I could go to the store and buy myself a pair of tennis shoes. But I thought this would give him something practical to get me. So I hinted around about what I wanted for Christmas. I didn't want that much. Really, we were talking one pair of shoes. My motives were very practical. I was trying to simplify things. Just buy me something I want. But on Christmas day, I didn't get anything. I was surprised and hurt.

When I asked him later why he didn't buy me anything, his logic was shocking. He told me that he went shopping looking for a special gift for me. He was looking for a mink coat. Now, where in his mind did a mink coat come in? I asked for tennis shoes.

Well, in going through the discussion on why he was looking for a mink coat, I realized how differently we think. Buying something really nice for me was his way of saying, "I know you work hard. And I know I ask a lot of you. And I wanted to give you something nice." But when he couldn't find an affordable luxury, he thought, "If I couldn't give you something nice, then I won't give you anything at all." And I remember lamenting, "All I *asked* for was a pair of tennis shoes."

Our Expectations of Others

We also expect others to meet our standards and to meet the commitments they make to us. Our high expectations lead us to expect big things from them. We are often disappointed.

Kate: The judge

Early in my career, I worked as a branch administrator in a regional sales office. The sales staff completed highly technical sales orders and then my staff processed and forwarded the orders to the corporate office each month. My standard was perfection. After all, that was in everyone's best interests, I thought. If the orders weren't perfect, my inventory was a nightmare, my branch didn't meet its profit-and-loss requirements, and the sales commissions were delayed. I felt the pressure for the branch to be successful.

At first, I personally fixed the errors, mountainous as they were. But that meant I worked at a frantic pace until late each night during the last week of the month. My resentment grew, not to mention my irritability factor. My stress level became unbearable, so I decided to stop carrying. But rather than communicating with the sales group and finding out why the orders were wrong, I started throwing the orders back to the sales people to fix. Quite literally, throwing them. At closeout, the nervous group would hang out at their desks, unable to go home, because if I tossed an order back to one of them to fix and he or she wasn't there, that person lost the commission for that month. They called me "The Judge" because my decisions were final and often harsh. But I didn't give an inch.

At Christmas, I got a mug from the sales director. It said "Bitch, bitch, bitch." I guess I deserved it. But I really didn't think perfection was too much to ask.

Joan: No trash, no love

When I married Allen, I was very independent and expected very little from others. But I did expect him to do what he said he would do. It wasn't necessary for Allen to tell me he loved me every day or to bring me roses. It wasn't a case of wishing he had sent me flowers and keeping quiet if he didn't. It just didn't occur to me that flowers were an expression of love. On the other hand, if he told me he was going to take out the trash, he had better do it. It was in the chores, the promises, that I measured love. If he didn't take out the trash, then I figured he didn't care.

Others' Expectations of Us

Another aspect of carrying is the way we set up others' expectations of us. We trap ourselves into a carrying role by volunteering to take on tasks (after all, who can do it better?) or bailing out others on such a regular basis that they quit doing the job altogether.

The messy room syndrome of many mothers is classic.

"When are you going to pick up this room?" we ask our twelve-year-old son or daughter.

"Tonight, after I get home from music . . . baseball practice . . . the open house . . . [fill in the blank]," they reply.

Next day, the room is one day messier, with another layer of clothes piled on the growing heap.

"If this room isn't clean by tomorrow, I'm going to [fill in the blank] . . . take away your allowance . . . ground you . . . hang you from your light fixture by your big toe," you say.

That night, the child has a soccer practice, followed by a major report. At 10:30 P.M., an hour past his regular bedtime, he falls into bed. You ignore the room.

Friday comes, and a friend is coming over. You get home from work and buzz through the house, making sure it fits your "company" standards. Your child is at a friend's house and when you get to his room, all your stated intentions about letting him rot in his garbage disappear. What has kicked in is your desire for your home to live up to your standards of acceptable cleanliness. So, you pick up the dirty clothes, take the crusted dishes back to the kitchen, throw away the chip and candy-bar wrappers, and straighten out the bed covers.

Has this happened before? For too many of us, the answer is yes.

It's no wonder our children never pick up their rooms. They know they can count on us to come through.

"Thanks, Mom," a disarming child will say. "I appreciate your cleaning up my room."

And although you may mutter, "Never again," the kids don't believe it, and, chances are, neither do you.

But it's not just our children we pick up after. As our expectations of ourselves rise, we often project these same expectations on others. This is dangerous. While our high standards for ourselves may, or may not, be appropriate, these same expectations placed on others are often totally unrealistic. That doesn't stop us, though. To move our agenda along, we find ourselves carrying other adults in order to accomplish the given task according to our standards. Before long, we are doing the job for them. Next? Well, quite realistically on their part, they expect us to take their load, as Marta and Michelle point out.

Marta: The 5 A.M. fruit trip

I really outdid myself on the expectations I set up among my family. They depended on me for every little item. In many ways, my husband was the worst. But, in retrospect, I can see how I set up his expectation that I would take care of all his needs.

I remember one particular evening. I was pregnant and my husband was feeling ill, so he slept on the downstairs couch. Suddenly, at 4:30 A.M. the phone rang. My phone upstairs wasn't working, so only the one downstairs was operational.

I'm thinking: It's between four and four-thirty in the morning, something terrible has happened. His grandmother. Oh, no, his grandmother has died. Or the alarm went off at the shop and the police were calling to say we had been robbed! At that time of the morning, what could it be? My heart was beating furiously as I ran down the stairs.

I went to grab the phone near my husband and he said, "You don't need to get that."

"Why not?" I asked.

"Because it's me," he replied.

I looked closer and saw his car phone in his hand. He had called me . . . scared me to death . . . gotten me out of bed.

"What's wrong?" I asked between clenched teeth.

"Can I have some fresh fruit?" he asked.

This man was lying on the couch in the family room, which was next to the kitchen. I wanted to throw something at him, but I also knew he was really feeling awful. So I restrained myself.

"What would you like, dear?" I asked, smoke coming out of my ears, but he was too sick to notice.

"Do you have any fresh pineapple?" he said.

"Have you known me ever to have fresh pineapple?" I replied. By this time, I was really getting angry. "Do you really want me working with a knife at four A.M.?" I said sarcastically.

But my husband, feeling awful, missed the sarcasm. Instead, he asked, "Do you have any good juices?"

"What do you mean, good juices?" I replied.

"You know, like the healthy kind," he said.

"What do you mean, the healthy kind?" I replied.

"Well, something besides the kids' juice in the little cardboard boxes," he said.

So at 5 A.M., I went to the twenty-four-hour grocery store shopping for fruit and juices. It was March, and the only fruits available were apples, oranges, and bananas. So I bought some of each, muttering questions like "Would you like me to import some fruit for you?" I bought a dozen different juices. I even bought popsicles. I must have spent $75 on juice and fruit. I was really angry, and I really didn't care what he liked. I just wanted to go back to bed, so I bought everything fruity I could find.

It didn't really matter. I knew he wouldn't like whatever I bought. He was too sick to have an appetite. But I got into this resentment mode: "How dare you put me through this, because when I'm sick, I have to keep going."

When I came back, I got him something to eat. And I sat, literally by the phone, on the chair and I looked at him. And he looked back. When he's sick, the world comes to an end. When I'm sick, I'm expected to keep going. I'm expected to still be nurturing. I'm expected to have control over everything. And it's not fair and it's not right, but I have to deal with it.

Michelle: Toilet paper, too

I used to wonder how I got to be the "mother hen" of the office, the one who would always bail out the salesman with a problem, the one who gave all the birthday and going-away parties, the one who kept the office supplied with toilet paper and paper cups. I guess I set it up. I just didn't realize I was doing it.

I had been the mother-confessor to guys at my high school. We were friends, and they would ask me how to get this or that girl's attention . . . things like that. We were buddies. I loved it. They respected me and respected my opinion. So, when I went to work, I did the same thing. I asked the salesmen in the office about their wives, their children. I kept up with them. Before long, they were dumping their problems on me. Since I was on dialysis, my whole life seemed to revolve around work and the clinic where I hooked up to the machine three times a week. So talking about *their* problems gave me something to do and care about.

But it was a short step from being friends to being asked to help them out on their work assignments. When some of them had trouble with their reporting forms, I jumped in to help. Pretty soon, they were *expecting* that help.

I volunteered to plan the first birthday party, too. In fact, it was my idea. One of the men's birthday was coming up, and I had found out about it. So I baked a cake, and brought in paper plates and a card for everyone to sign. When the next birthday arrived, someone asked if I was going to bake that "great chocolate cake again." Sure, I replied. Soon, I had the unofficial title of "Birthday Lady."

I volunteered once to go to the discount store and get sundry stuff that we needed for the office, such as toilet paper. No one liked the hard, crinkly tissue provided by the office building management. It wasn't long before I claimed another unofficial title: "Supply Lady."

It wasn't easy to keep up this pace. At one point, I was getting sicker and sicker. But no one's expectations of me changed, including, I suppose, my own. I can remember more than once rushing to the discount store to buy supplies, having left the office later than I should, on my way to the clinic to hook up for six hours.

So, I just kept adding to my duties and people came to expect it, I guess. I was the office's counselor *plus* the party giver and supply quartermaster, the problem solver, and the unofficial human resource department.

Joan: Honey, come here

So often, when I talked to Allen, it was to ask if he had done a task he had already consented to do. I was always monitoring him like a parent. It struck me on one occasion how that behavior might be perceived from his viewpoint.

I was watching television. We had a big ice storm that day, and the television crew had taken some remarkable footage of a sand truck sliding into a curb and creaming a little sports car parked by the curb. There was other footage, too, of a city bus sliding sideways down the street. My husband enjoyed watching the weather report, and I immediately realized he would get a real kick out of this dramatic footage. So, I called, "Honey, come here!"

He didn't come. Later, I was telling him about the wintry scenes and asked him why he didn't respond.

"I figured you were just going to ask me if I had called the accountant. I hadn't, so I didn't see any reason to respond," he said.

Suddenly, I got a clear picture of his view of me. He expected me to always be "on him" for one reason or another. So he quit responding.

Smart women who carry begin with high expectations—of ourselves, of others, of life. Meeting these expectations is our challenge. To do so, we often feel we must take control, not only of our own life, but of those around us whose lives we believe impact our own. The issue of control stands like a giant neon warning light that we have crossed the line from caring into carrying.

Characteristics of Women Who Carry

These are some of the common characteristics of women who carry at home, with friends, or at work:

- High expectations of self
- High expectations of others
- Tendency to take control
- Attempting to fix whatever is wrong
- Demanding perfection in how things are accomplished
- Expecting completion of tasks within own time frame
- A low-maintenance personality
- Extreme independence
- Commitment to her relationships at all costs
- Commitment at work regardless of requirements

Your Story

What characteristics of carrying do you see in yourself?

Reflect on your answers to Questions 1 and 2 of the Survey in Chapter One.

1. I expect others to:

2. I expect myself to:

What expectations of yourself may be too high?

What expectations do you have of others that may be too high?

Chapter 4
Signs You Have Crossed the Line

Over time, our desire to see our high expectations met turns into control. Control is the illusion that we can make everything happen to perfection if we keep a firm grip on the reins. We really don't trust anyone but ourselves to get the job done. As we take over the controls, either subtly or overtly, we begin to carry. We cross the line from helping someone to carrying them. Soon we find we are overcommitted. Even we can't do it all. The end result is exhaustion.

Does the following list sound familiar?

The vacation? If we don't plan it, it doesn't happen. So we get out the calendars, block out the dates, call the travel agent, or take the car in to be serviced. We research the best prices, what to do at our destination, figure out the budget. We inventory what we need, make the shopping trip for clothes or sundries, pack the bags. Then, by the time the vacation starts, we are exhausted.

Child care? We do it. We keep the family schedule and inform our husbands or helpers when and where to transport the children if we can't get away from work to do it ourselves. Because we don't trust anyone to remember the schedule, we call thirty minutes early to remind them.

Household finances? At some point, we discovered our spouses would overspend and lose control of the checkbook, and we would get "insufficient funds" notices from our banks. We don't trust them to keep up with the quarterly income-tax payments, because, quite frankly, they let it go in the past before we took over. So we pay the bills, reconcile the checking account, worry about the budget, put our husbands on an allowance, and cut back on credit cards.

Home maintenance? We handle those projects, too. At midnight, we are doing laundry. On Saturdays, we are mowing the lawn and cleaning. We call the plumber and the appliance-repair service. We track the periodic maintenance due on our air-conditioning and heating units and call for service.

Extended family? We keep up with them also. We schedule when to visit the in-laws and our parents, and plan the trips. We remind our husbands to call their parents. When the in-laws visit, we plan the meals, cook the food, and organize the recreational outings.

Career? Yes, we do that too. Our husbands can't always be counted on to provide financially, either. They have changed jobs too often, and let us down when we most needed the support. We can't rely on them to provide continuous funds. So we pursue our careers with a fervor, work late, and take courses to advance us up the ranks.

Coworkers? Many of us take our controlling impulses to work. We know our idea is the best, so we take over—making sure each detail is carried out to our specifications, either by doing it ourselves or constantly monitoring the work of an employee who is handling the details while we "manage" the project. Either way, our desire for control keeps us carrying a disproportionate share of the work load and keeps our office lights shining late into the night.

It's a lose-lose situation. We overcommit, then resort to avoidance or cave in to exhaustion.

The signs you are carrying may seem like smart choices, but they are really red flags. And none is a brighter red than the tendency to control.

Taking Control

As high-expectation women, we have a tendency to take control. We believe no one but us can do the task right, whatever it is. This attitude is a major culprit that leads us to cross the line between caring and carrying.

Marta: Just in case

I have always wanted the sequence of events around me to flow perfectly. I want to be the perfect employee, the perfect wife, the perfect mother. So I went way beyond the call of duty.

My job required me to take about two trips a month. Usually the trips were three to four days—occasionally a full week. I would spend days preparing everything my family would need while I was gone, down to the smallest detail, and then some.

I would do all the laundry before I left. But I did more than just make sure everyone had clean clothes. I laid out all the children's clothes for each day. The three oldest were in a private school and wore uniforms, so you'd think it would be easy for my husband to do, but only I knew the schedule—on which days they needed to take their gym clothes and wear tennis shoes, on which day Tina's ballet class met and where her leotard and shoes were, on which days James needed his soccer clothes. I'd lay out all the items and label them according to day. To keep their lives on track, I even laid out underclothes and socks. I felt that everything had to run perfectly, and only I could do it.

I would also go to the grocery store and buy food, which I would cook and freeze before I left. I would leave a note for my husband telling him what to pack for each child's lunch that week. I would either prepare or buy easy-to-prepare meals and leave my husband instructions on what to do for each dinner. Half the time when I came home I would find out they had eaten fast food anyway, but I still prepared every meal—just in case.

Once I stocked only food for the lunches, knowing my husband would take the children out for dinner. Upon my return he commented, "You left me with no bread." I had set my family up to expect everything from me. I had crossed the line between caring and carrying.

Sarah: Fix it up

I am a fixer. Every time Marvin complained, I tried to fix the situation. I even let him quit his jobs in the hope that he would quit complaining if he had a new one. I always rationalized that next time he would be happy. Well, he never was. Something was always wrong—his boss was a jerk, the company policies were stupid, it didn't pay enough, the hours were too long. There was always a reason the job was terrible.

For twenty-five years, I kept trying to make life easier for Marvin. Every time he complained about how hard or unfair life was, I would step in to make everything better. Marvin's foray into entrepreneurship was a classic example. A mechanic during much of his working life, Marvin decided he wanted his own business. He wanted to be a real-estate appraiser.

"Okay, do that," I encouraged.

The excuses started. "I don't have the right certification," he explained. "I really can't compete with all the regional and national firms. . . ."

True to form, I began to "fix" each objection. I called a well-known real-estate school and applied to get Marvin certified. I also paid the fees. I helped him study for his certification test. I did everything but take the damn test for him.

After Marvin became certified, I called my friends and recruited several as clients for Marvin. I kept thinking that if Marvin were happy, then we would be happy.

But Marvin wasn't happy. He quickly needed more clients, and he wanted me to bring in more business. I was working full time and carrying the household responsibilities. I couldn't be Marvin's full-time sales force. But I didn't quit offering solutions. I suggested he hire someone on a commission basis to find clients.

Instead, Marvin quit the business. He had become dependent on my nurturing help. He just couldn't go it alone. In Marvin's mind, it became my fault the business failed because I wouldn't help him enough. He depended on me to control the process. Over the course of many years, I had set him up to expect everything from me. I had crossed the line.

I did the same at work. I let my coworkers hand off their work for me to finish. I would be at work until 9 or 10 P.M. Everyone else would have left by 5 or 6 P.M. They would come in and say, "I can't get this out," or "I have a problem," or "I don't know how to do this." I'd just take it on, whatever it was, and send them home.

I can remember once taking a team project and working until 3 A.M. on it. When the "team" came in the next day, they were very surprised. They examined the project, and immediately began to find fault. But I patiently answered all their concerns, explaining why I had taken each step. Finally, they signed off on it. The "team" project was complete. Only it wasn't a team project at all. It was *my* project. I just let them take credit with me. I had crossed the line again.

Joan: Monitor madness

Even though I knew I would be the main financial support when I married Allen, I was unprepared for his procrastination tendencies. I became a nag, really. I would ask Allen to do something, such as figure out why the hubcaps on the car were rattling.

"It's because they need to be tightened," he would reply. That job required jacking up the car, taking off the wheels, and tightening the hubcaps.

"Would you do that?" I might ask.

"Sure," he would reply. But he didn't really mean it. Weeks came and went. And the car would still rattle.

I would find myself asking repeatedly, "Are you going to tighten the hubcaps?"

"Yes," he would reply. But he didn't. Before long, whenever he told me he would do something, I didn't really believe him. So, I would keep monitoring, asking if the job had been done.

I was just as bad in my business. I delegated tasks, but I'm sure I drove people crazy because I was always asking what they'd found out, what had happened, what was going on with this or that item. I know they felt I was checking up on them constantly. Delegating was not a problem for me. Letting loose and trusting them to get the job done without constant interference was the problem.

Making All the Money Decisions

For smart women, controlling money is another major red flag. Consider the surprising insight of my business associate, Sue. She is a senior vice president at a food-service company, and she was telling me about the rough seas her marriage was encountering. Sue had unexpectedly become the chief breadwinner, and that caused big trouble.

Sue told me that originally she planned to stay home after she and her husband, John, an upscale interior designer, had children. Neither of their mothers had worked when John and Sue were growing up. After marriage, Sue went to work and discovered she loved it. She loved the feeling of success. She worked for a progressive company with great employees, the kind of place where everyone dressed up for Halloween and had impromptu parties at the end of the day. It was fun, and she didn't want to quit.

After eight years of marriage, Sue and John changed their idyllic game plan. They decided they *could* both work and have children. Three babies came in quick succession. Then John's business went belly-up when the economy collapsed, and people quit building the million-dollar homes he was well known for decorating. At the same time, Sue's career took off as she moved into the executive ranks. Suddenly, Sue became the primary breadwinner. John moved his business home and was soon picking up more and more of the child-rearing duties.

Over time, Sue took complete financial control. It wasn't deliberate, just expedient. John's artistic, free-spirited nature was averse to basic bookkeeping. At first, he kept the family checkbook. He totally messed it up. Checks were bouncing everywhere. After just one month, Sue fired him. She took over. As time went on, she gradually took over more and more of the financial decisions. But one particular incident really brought the lesson home to Sue, and the impact it was having on their fifteen-year marriage.

"Before many years passed, everything was in my name," she told me. "I didn't realize what a hard pill this was for John to swallow until recently. We were paying an annual fee on an American Express Gold Card, and I suggested John cancel it.

"'We don't need to pay this charge,' I said.

"But John adamantly refused. I was thinking this was a status symbol he didn't want to discard. I brought the subject up again a month or two later.

"Finally, he said, 'This is the only credit card we have in *my* name.'

"I hadn't thought about that. All of the cars and credit cards were in my name. When did that happen, I wonder now?"

Without thinking about it, without planning for it to happen,

Sue gained complete financial control for a family of five. Little wonder that the relationship was going through tough times.

Women who are the principal breadwinner find themselves carrying the responsibilities of buying the house, the car, and the groceries, often making the decisions on how the leftover money is spent. Most of them did not start their marriages thinking this is what would happen. For many women, such as Sue, taking monetary control was a subtle process over time. For others, such as Michelle, the relationship began that way.

Michelle: Money mama

I controlled the money from the start of our marriage. I had a house. I bought the cars. I paid the bills. Lionel worked only sporadically—construction jobs. In that way, he was free to play with his band when the opportunity arose. Most of his money went to maintaining his image. Lionel always needed three hundred dollars in his pocket, while twenty bucks of pocket change was enough for me. But Lionel felt that when the time came to buy drinks with his friends, he should be able to roll out a big wad of bills. To him, that was success. He dressed well, too—expensive, two-toned leather shoes, hats, double-breasted suits, colored shirts and ties that changed with the seasons.

I wanted him to take more monetary responsibility. At one point, I goaded him into taking a full-time position at a food company. But when the band began to get air time on the local radio station and the bookings picked up, he quit again.

So I continued to pay the bills and the mortgage. I also kept a savings account that he knew nothing about. That was my safety net in case I got sick and ended up in the hospital again for an extended period. Maintaining the basic necessities of life was my responsibility, so I just went ahead and managed the money and made the decisions that kept our home intact.

Kate: Never mind

Well, I knew when we married that Richard wasn't responsible with a checkbook and that I would handle that part of our finances. But I still thought our marriage would be more of a partnership than it was. I gradually began to make all of the financial decisions.

At first, I expected him to take care of various responsibilities. I often found that what I thought he was going to do, he hadn't done at all. On one occasion, for example, he volunteered to drop a check I had written for our electric bill in the payment window at the electric company near where he worked.

"This is great." I beamed, thinking he was assuming more responsibility.

It seemed a simple-enough task. But he forgot. He never took the envelope out of his pocket. I didn't realize there was a problem until I got a notice from the electric company threatening to cut off our services. So I began monitoring things.

When nothing improved, I quit asking him to do even simple things. I just began to do them myself. It was easier. In a way, it was a self-preservation move on my part. I saved myself the stress of having to monitor him and be disappointed.

So Richard was no longer actively helping. But then he began not wanting even to participate in the decision-making process. He didn't want to be involved at all in buying the house, or buying the car, or picking out furniture. At first, I would ask him what he thought or ask him to go along to look at something I was considering purchasing. But he would turn me down.

"Whatever you decide is fine," he said.

Finally, I just thought, "Never mind." I went and bought whatever we needed without mentioning it to him.

It made life easier for me. He was easy to please. He never complained about my choices. He just didn't want to be involved.

Carrying Other Family Members

And then there is the family connection. Since our standards are high, we can be counted on to come through for family, too. After all, we already have proven our capability in many ways.

Tamara: Taking care of Mom . . . and Dad . . . and Sis . . .

I come from a large family, six children in all. As the oldest girl, I helped out from an early age with my younger brothers and sisters. Being there for family was always a priority. When Phil and I were married, taking on *his* family's problems seemed normal. But those problems, added on to my family's challenges, were enormous.

Taking care of his alcoholic mother proved to be too much early in our marriage. I was sympathetic to her problems, but her temper tantrums and outbursts caused a lot of stress. Phil finally had to find another place for her.

Then, Phil's father became ill and we took him in. We have a separate apartment for him over the garage. He is a recluse and keeps to himself, but we go up to visit every day, each of us watching certain TV programs with him.

My own large family has its shares of ups and downs—marital problems, money problems, aging parents, the usual gamut in a group that large. When one of my sisters has financial or relationship problems, she always ends up at our house, sometimes for weeks or even months. I am the family sounding board and homeless shelter.

I knew I had crossed the line when two of my sisters were temporarily living with us, along with Phil's father. My sisters had the girls' room, and the girls were on sleeping bags in the living room. No one had any privacy. After two weeks, we were all on edge. When one sister started complaining about the mattress on the bed hurting her back, Phil and I knew something had to change in our family relationships.

Marta: Too many balls

It's a natural part of my style to care for people. So, as my parents began to age, I naturally began to care for them. Both my sister and I help them, but because I have always been the take-charge person, they rely on me more than on my sister. I believe my sister gives them a limit on what they may or may not ask for. I just say, "Okay, Dad, okay, Mom, I'll take care of that," anytime they ask for anything. So if my dad asks me to call the tree trimmer service, I'm on the phone calling the tree trimmer. Or, then again, maybe I'm not. The truth is, I get so busy I don't have time to call. I've had to realize I can't do everything. Too many balls are going "splat" these days.

Like my mother and the doctor. My mom had a female problem. I told her I would set up an appointment with her gynecologist. Well, it was the usual busy week at work and at home. I called the doctor, left a message. He called back, and left a message for me. Two days later, I called again. Next day, he calls back. I'm not in my office. He leaves a message. A week goes by and no appointment has been scheduled for my suffering mom. I'm just too busy to keep up with it all, in spite of my good intentions.

Kate: Twelve children?

By the time Richard and I were married a few years, I had added most of his family to my list of people to take care of. I was used to the responsibility of family, so it seemed natural to add Richard's family to that list.

His four sisters listed me in their wills as guardian of their children should they die prematurely. That's the level of trust I generated, and I was honored. There was no doubt in anyone's mind that I would take on the responsibility and treat it seriously. But I didn't think about the implications had something really happened—I would have been the proud mother of twelve children!

Richard's older sister became an ongoing financial burden. She was a single parent with two small children and she worked as a waitress. She often came to me the day after rent was due or the day before her car was going to be repossessed and asked for money. We had plenty, so it seemed easy to say yes, but her situation never improved. I guess there was no real reason for her to change it. She always got what she needed.

It didn't stop there. Even after Richard and I were separated, when his youngest sister had marital problems, she came to stay with me, not Richard. I was the one who shored her up.

Meanwhile, my own family was requiring a lot of attention. My parents divorced and my sister was hurt in a car wreck. So I added the roles of legal adviser, emotional therapist, and medical monitor to my list of "services" for them. It's little wonder that at the speed I was operating, I finally burned out.

Reba: Never-ending motherhood

I know I still carry two of my four adult children. I had one birth son, Peter. He was born thirteen weeks premature and weighed only two pounds. Nobody thought he would live. It was truly a miracle he did. He had all kinds of damages resulting from this very premature birth, including a blindness in the focal point of his eyes that led to his being incredibly uncoordinated. Teaching him to drive was undoubtedly the bravest act I ever pulled off. It was always hard to know what he could or couldn't do. I always did way too much for him, because I was afraid that I was asking too much of him. So, he still depends on me far too much for a grown man.

Our other three children came to me when I married their father. Their mother was an alcoholic and on welfare. Our twin daughters, Kathy and Kerri, came to live with us right after we were married. They were nine years old. We quickly became very close. Both of them modeled themselves after me. They were soon independent and self-sufficient.

Their older sister didn't come to live with us until she was fifteen. Darlene was a street kid, living in a ghetto neighborhood, tough and old beyond her years. She has never quite gotten a true picture of the world. She wanted to be a model, so she started a small talent agency. But we are always having to help her out financially.

The twins, though, are self-sufficient and have taken over some of the care-giving. When I am out of town, their older brother and sister lean on them.

Overstepping the Boundaries of Friendship

We often overstep the boundaries of friendship, taking over responsibility for our friends' lives, once again trying to make everything all right. It's an attempt to make their lives as productive as ours.

Joan: Adopting Helen

Adopting other people comes naturally. Raised in a family with plenty of income, my mother always told us we should help others less fortunate. She did. I knew she helped others and gave away clothes and furniture by the truckload, but only after she died did I realize how many children she had put through college in addition to us. We kept getting sympathy cards from people telling us how she had helped them. Anyway, I suppose that's where I got this strong need to help others.

I was always willing to lend money to friends. I never kept track of it. Some paid me back. Some didn't. I couldn't tell you who did or didn't. I never tracked it. I also took in friends when they needed a place to stay for a while. Some stayed a few weeks, some a few months.

The worst was Helen. Helen and I had been college roommates, best friends for several years. A few years ago, she was facing a real dilemma. She held the title of chief financial officer for a small company, but realized she hated the work.

Meanwhile, my business was really expanding and I needed someone to help handle my growing client list. We began to talk and I suggested she join my business, taking the title of president (I was CEO). Helen had never been involved in public relations before, but she was willing to try.

Her husband, Jake, an aspiring artist, decided to move to California. She was carrying him. So, being ever helpful, I began to carry Helen. I suggested she move in with us for a while until Jake got established, and Helen could join him.

I began to teach her the business. At first, it was great. I felt so good, helping her learn and seeing her improve. She was very enthusiastic. She learned fast. Anyway, I already knew how smart Helen was.

Because we were friends as well as business associates, and even roommates again, I felt obligated to include her in everything. When Allen and I went on a short vacation, I invited Helen. I didn't want her to feel like an outsider, and I knew she couldn't afford to go on her own. Allen put up with it, but the whole arrangement baffled him. Since I was spending my money, however, he just kind of shook his head and said little.

Helen lived with us for two years. Before it was all over, our friendship was in tatters. Understanding my role in that severed relationship was to be a real lesson for me.

Reba: Taking care of Jenny

Twenty years later, Jenny is still my good friend. As single moms in college, living in subsidized housing, I needed her to be my friend, and she needed me to survive.

I always made sure she was financially okay. Sometimes, our meager paychecks wouldn't make it through the month. So I found the odd jobs that got us through, like picking up glass bottles and returning them for the deposit. I studied with her and made sure she passed. Later, when we graduated and were on our feet, I went to her house closing, doing the paperwork for her, helping her pack, finding the movers, helping her unpack. We have always had that kind of relationship.

In college, I took it upon myself to keep her employed. Jenny really wasn't a responsible person. She wouldn't get up in the morning and get to work on time. It drove me crazy. We *had* to keep these jobs, because we had to support our two children. And Jenny would never get up. She'd set fourteen alarm clocks and not wake up.

Well, not too surprisingly, her boss was threatening to fire her if she was late again.

"One more time late and you are toast," he told her.

I was really worried, practically hysterical. I just knew it was going to happen. And sure enough, one morning soon after, I called to make sure she was up (I always called). She wasn't gone. She was in bed. She answered very sleepily.

"Jenny," I shouted. "You've got to be at work!"

"No . . ." she muttered and hung up.

I could tell she wasn't getting up. Desperate, I called her office.

"Hello. Is Mr. Smith in?" I asked. "This is Rosemont Community Hospital."

When Mr. Smith answered, I pretended to be the admittance clerk calling to confirm that she worked there. I explained to him that Jenny didn't have her insurance card on her and we were very concerned. I asked him if she worked there, and whether she was covered. It was actually a very clever ruse.

But she eventually got fired anyway. This was the late 1960s, and Jenny was still busy making love beads. She wouldn't look for work. So I supported both of us—four of us, actually—for several months until I finally convinced her to answer one of the want ads I was constantly putting in front of her.

But Jenny wasn't the only one. I've adopted others over the years. I always figured I could find answers for everyone.

Disruptions in Intimate Relationships

Most relationships start out with that magical ingredient we call "chemistry" between the sexes. But as the responsibilities shift out of balance, what started out as a playful, reciprocal sexual relationship disappears. This loss of physical intimacy between couples is difficult for both the man and the woman. Sometimes, it plants the seed for infidelity.

Sarah: The other women

Marvin and I married because of lust. After all, we were barely out of high school. At the beginning of our marriage the sex was great. I got pregnant right away. After his return from Vietnam, the sex play picked right back up.

But, as I began to make more and more decisions and became a parent, all that changed. I made romantic efforts, setting up candlelit dinners on occasion, making sure birthdays and anniversaries were special. But for me, sex had diminished to an occasional biological need. I tried to pretend that was enough. We still made love occasionally, but Marvin was finding sexual playmates outside the marriage.

The first time I discovered his unfaithfulness, I threw him out. We had been married ten years. And I was definitely making all the decisions by then. He moved into an apartment around the corner and courted me for six months. He called every day, sent me flowers and cards, and pleaded for another chance. I took him back.

But after we moved again because of my promotion, he must have started being unfaithful again. He went clubbing with friends I never met. In retrospect, I think many of them might have been women. But I was working so hard I was, quite frankly, too tired to care. I just kept plugging away. On increasingly rare occasions, I would set up a romantic date. We would make love on those nights.

But the end came after almost twenty-five years of marriage. I could ignore his infidelity no longer. I found two tickets to a show in his jacket pocket. The date was Mother's Day. Although I didn't really think so deep down, I hoped that perhaps he was planning to surprise me. On Mother's Day, I was especially sweet, taking care not to say anything that would start an argument.

At six o'clock, Marvin announced, "We've been together all day. I am going to go out with the guys for a while."

"I'll come with you," I said, uncharacteristically. "I have nothing else to do now."

He tried a couple of other tacks, but when I wouldn't let him go gracefully, he resorted to accusations.

"Why do you have to be a noose around my neck!" he shouted as he left the house.

I knew by now, of course, that those tickets were for him and another woman. I drove to the theater after he left to confront him, but the show was sold out. I saw his car and contemplated smashing his windshield. But violence was never my style. I wrote a very nasty note. Finally, I calmed down and wrote a short note. It said, "Hope you enjoyed the show. Don't bother to come home. I changed the security code."

He was on the phone the next day, quietly pleading for forgiveness. I spent twenty-five years caring for Marvin. It was hard to shut that down. I knew I shouldn't, but on that day, I took him back again.

Tamara: Lost chemistry

The chemistry between Phil and me was magic. We had sex several times a day in the beginning of our relationship. It was pretty incredible. I thought of us primarily as spiritual soul mates, not just physical ones. The combination of the two dimensions was dynamite for both of us.

But that lasted as long as Phil was pulling his weight. When he wouldn't do his share of the chores, and then wouldn't even keep up his end of the bargain in our business, I turned off. The more responsibility I took on, the less I wanted sex. Phil still wanted to make love, but I thought of it simply as an obligation. If enough time had passed, I would consent solely because I felt I had to. But I didn't really enjoy it. I don't think he did either.

As time went on and I became more and more disillusioned with our marriage, even that ended. We weren't playmates any longer.

Staying Busy to Avoid

Some of us, like Sarah, began to avoid facing the stack of issues we have before us. Sarah was constantly late, always running behind as she tried to finish one more item on her list.

Sarah: Honey, I have to work late . . . again

My friends might wait for two hours for me to show up for dinner. Needless to say, I probably lost a few in the process. I was a good avoider. I avoided facing the fact that I probably wouldn't get everything done. I avoided facing my declining marital relationship with Marvin. I avoided it all. When I was asked to join a board, or do another work project, I always said yes. I never had a clue how it might get done. I just figured it would all work out. As for home, well, work became a way to avoid coming face-to-face with my home life.

My marriage was a mess. Marvin and I basically fought over everything. I tuned out his whining and complaining. But it never occurred to me to face the fact that I had a rotten marriage. I had said "I do" for better or worse. It appeared that the "worse" part was winning out, so I took to avoiding the situation, rather than confronting it.

Work was a perfect excuse not to go home. There was never any shortage of work to do. And since I was so willing to do others' work, I could easily put in twelve- to fourteen-hour days and still leave a pile on my desk to be tackled the next day. I got all my support, all my encouragement from friends at work. There I was needed; but even better, I was appreciated. I got lots of compliments for my work. Once our daughter graduated from high school, coming home at 10 or 11 P.M. was not unusual for me. I didn't even realize I was avoiding the situation at home. I thought I *had* to work late.

Overcommitment

The result of carrying is overcommitment. We simply cannot do it all. But it takes some of us quite a while to realize that. We just naturally say "Yes," because we know we can do the job. And we can. The problem lies in taking on so much that we can't keep all the balls in the air simultaneously.

I remember one incident in which I began to get a glimmer of these limitations. My husband and I often had small dinner parties. I enjoyed cooking. We planned such a party for several of our family members for one weekend. I flew in Friday from a consulting job on the West Coast. Friday night, I started getting ready for the party.

First, I had to clean the house. I knew that other women would notice that layer of dirt on the baseboards, so, already exhausted from my week's trip, I went to work with dust mop and spray cleaner in hand. I got up early the next morning to go grocery shopping for that night's menu. Then I got a clear sign I was on overload. Preparing the food that afternoon, I suddenly realized we had no pepper, and I basically became hysterical. My husband came in, and I was sobbing.

"What's wrong?" he asked, with some concern.

"We're [sob] out of [sob] pepper!" I cried.

Running back to the store to get pepper was a small chore, but at that moment it was the proverbial straw that broke the old camel's back.

"Hattie," I said to myself the next day as I lay in bed too exhausted to get up. "You need to let go of giving dinner parties. You can't do it all."

I'm not the only one who tried and failed.

Joan: Guilt if I do, guilt if I don't

Man, what a dilemma! Here I was, stuck between two bad decisions. I had served two years out of a three-year assignment on the board of a shelter for abused women. Since accepting the board assignment, I had started a new business that was taking up much of my time. This was a working board, not an honorary one. It took everyone's effort to keep this shelter funded. The second year I served on the board, I felt guilty for the little time I put into that effort. I attended every other board meeting, and did some extra work on the fund-raising side, but not nearly enough to ease my conscience. Now I was facing this dilemma: either quit the board a year earlier than scheduled and feel guilty about not meeting my commitment, or stay on the board, but feel guilty about not doing enough to help out. It looked like a lose-lose situation from my vantage point. Either way I felt guilty.

Tamara: The self-employment dilemma

I think many of us who are self-employed carry our customers. I know I have.

Carrying works like this: I give a proposal to a prospective client. The company sits on it for months. It is simply not unusual in my experience for the client to procrastinate on making a decision.

Then, out of the blue, the person calls, and says the company has decided to go ahead, and has accepted my proposal. And they expect the work to be turned around instantaneously. They give me an almost impossible deadline.

Now, I am caught between two options. Do I kill myself meeting this deadline because I really want the money? Or do I tell them I can't meet the deadline? I almost always say yes to their demands.

Now, I am under intense pressure. I am trying to meet this near-impossible deadline, but my standards aren't any lower. I want the work I produce to be beyond their expectations. I want the company to be happy. So, I work all night, on weekends, and drive myself to tears doing their project on their deadline.

That's a kind of corporate carrying for the company's procrastination. It's the company that doesn't make a decision on the job until it is too late to do it on a reasonable work schedule. But once again I assume responsibility that really isn't mine.

The end result of carrying is exhaustion. The burden becomes too great. We can't walk another step carrying the responsibility for other adults on our shoulders. For many women carriers, this is the end of the relationship. For others, the lucky ones, it is the beginning of a changed perspective. It is time to make smart choices.

But before that end, we struggle on . . . and on . . . and on. . . .

The Signs of Carrying

There are many red-flag behaviors that alert you to carrying in your relationships. For example, you:

- Parent your spouse
- Manage the money
- Make all the decisions
- Stay busy to avoid facing the issues
- Assume responsibilities of other family members
- Overstep the boundaries of friendship
- Experience changes in your sexual relationship
- Quit asking for help
- Overcommit
- Feel burdened and exhausted
- Have a life that is unbalanced among work, family, social, personal, and spiritual needs

Your Story

What red flags indicate that you are carrying family members?

What red flags indicate that you are carrying friends?

What red flags indicate that you are carrying others at work?

Reflect on your answers to Questions 3, 4, and 5 of the Survey in Chapter One.

3. I take control when:

4. I'll take care of:

5. I don't take care of:

In what current situations have you taken too much control?

What things do you expect yourself to take care of that indicate you are carrying?

What things do you need to take care of that you don't take care of now?

Chapter 5
The Cycle of Carrying: The Four R's

For some of us, it takes a short time to realize a relationship is not going to work if we take on all the responsibility. For others, it is a cycle—a clear pattern—that repeats itself many times before we realize that our relationships are going downhill. For too many of us, the cycle speeds up from a slow spiral into a whirling vortex before we're sucked under and exhaust our will or ability to carry.

I call this cycle the Four R's. The R's stand for rationalization, reoccurrence, resolve, and resentment. Let's look at each of them separately.

Rationalization

The first mental step we take to begin carrying in a given situation is to rationalize why it's better for *us* to take on the particular responsibility. We have such high expectations of ourselves. Who can do it better? My travel planning illustrates this.

I planned all our trips and vacations in my marriage. I rationalized that it made sense for me to do this, because of my extensive business travel. I had all the connections. I had the free airline tickets from my frequent-flyer mileage. I knew the travel agents. I was familiar with the hotels. All of this was true. But in the process, my husband and I were no longer operating as a team, making joint decisions on vacations. I was planning the entire trip.

Reoccurrence

Soon, we find that whatever rationalization started us on this road, the process keeps happening again and again, long after the initial reasoning doesn't fit.

In my case, I even found myself planning trips in which I didn't need to be involved. When my husband and I were first married, we returned to his hometown every year for his annual family reunion. In the beginning of our marriage, my husband made all the arrangements. Generally, we stayed with his parents. Often we drove. But even if we were on a tight schedule and needed to fly, he called and booked the flight. For my husband, this was the equivalent of Christmas. He never missed it.

At some point, I took over the process. I was booking the flight. As we became more affluent, I was booking a hotel also, rather than staying with my husband's parents. It certainly wasn't an event I needed to take over. This was my husband's annual event.

Resolve

Some smart women never get to step three. As the pattern becomes apparent, they stop. But for many of us, *resolve* sets the stage for the reoccurring pattern. We resolve to see this job done, even if we are committing for a lifetime. Our rationalization process leads us into thinking that control is the easiest way to handle the situation. Short term, that is probably true. Long term, we all lose.

By the time I was married five years, I resolved that I would always plan the trip, regardless of where we were going. I had taken over. And my husband was glad to have me take over. It was one less item on his list of responsibilities.

Resentment

Resentment is sneaky. Despite having deliberately resolved to do this job, we often find a quiet resentment creeping in that we didn't count upon. For me, I began to resent doing everything. And it played two ways. My husband, even as he relinquished responsibility, resented having his individual rights usurped. In effect, he had given up power and autonomy.

My growing resentment about the imbalance of responsibilities in our marriage boiled over one fateful year before the annual family reunion. I was tired of making all the travel arrangements. I resented always having to think about where we were going next and what we were going to do once we got there.

That year, I simply didn't plan the trip. I didn't tell my husband. I just didn't lift a finger. By the time my husband realized it, it was too late to make hotel and flight arrangements. To say he was angry would be an understatement. In my husband's mind, missing the family reunion was not an option. The fight that ensued was not pretty.

We called the family to say hello but never discussed the reunion. His silence on the subject was indicative of his anger. Afterwards, I returned to the old cycle. I rationalized that, indeed, we should have been there, and resolved to make the arrangements well in advance for the next year. I just swallowed the resentment. And so, the process repeated itself in an endless loop.

Many of the other women were caught in the same loop—at home, with family, with friends, or at work.

Family and the Four R's
Joan and Allen: The major stonewaller

From day one, I rationalized that I didn't need financial support. I knew Allen was pretty naive about the amount of money it took to support us. But that was all right with me. I saw his wonderful qualities. He was loving and supportive of my ambitions and willing to support me emotionally, and he had a wonderful sense of humor. Being with him was always fun.

I also rationalized that when we had a child, his ambitions would rev up. He had a master's degree and all the credentials for success. We agreed to have one child, although I wasn't anxious to start a new family. My own children were just reaching the age—ten and twelve years old—where they didn't require constant care. I was looking forward to the end of the search for good baby-sitters. But Allen wanted a child. I thought that if he was willing to be a stepfather to my children, the least I could do was give him a child that would call him "Daddy" instead of "Allen." So we agreed to have another child.

But when Angela was born, the employment situation was no better for Allen. He kept hitting dead-end jobs. We remained dependent on my income. The cycle continued. So I resolved that I was indeed the family breadwinner. It was up to me. I started my own business to build the company I originally thought my husband might build. The resentment came out in my control. Since I was the chief financial support, I felt entitled to make all the financial decisions and to delegate duties at home. But we weren't a team. Allen's resentment came out in subtle ways. If I asked him to do a chore, like fix the garage door, he would say "Yes" and then just not do it. Weeks would pass. Nothing would happen. He became the master stonewaller.

This was the cycle. We were definitely in a slow, downward spiral, not really facing the issues.

Michelle and Lionel: But he's a good man

As a dialysis patient, I thought I would never have a lover or a companion. To have found one in Lionel was a miracle to me. So financially, I agreed to carry the load from the beginning. It was my house, bought before we were married. I paid the bills.

And Lionel wanted me to carry the load financially. That was fine with him. But that meant I also carried a lot of power. And that wasn't fine with his friends on the street. They would say, "How come you let your old lady keep all the cash?" "How come you let your woman do this . . . or do that?" So I guess that ate at him. The resentment started building.

My sickness made things even harder. Dialysis weakens a person in many ways. I was in the hospital a lot for various problems, including a hysterectomy, glaucoma surgery, and a kidney transplant, which later failed. That failure was a terrible blow for me. My friends would come to visit me, and say, "Where's Lionel? Why are we here to visit you and he isn't? Kick his butt out, Michelle." When he wasn't there for my illnesses, my resentment grew. I thought somehow he might take more responsibility when I was sick. But he didn't. If he did show up, it was generally to bring me the bills, so that I could pay them from my hospital bed.

But I was *resolved* with a capital R. Lionel was my friend before he was my lover and husband. "He's a good man," I rationalized to my friends. I never talked to Lionel about it. And so the cycle continued.

Marta and Joe: He works seven days a week

Joe comes home after he's put in a long day and plays couch potato. That's his way of bringing his mind and soul back into perspective again. So he pops in a movie or watches some old rerun. But when I come home I'm tending to the children. I'm cooking dinner and starting laundry.

I'm thinking of a thousand details that need to be taken care of, such as, today is Tuesday. The trash must go out tonight for pickup in the morning. Tomorrow is PE day, so I must make sure Jake's gym suit is clean. I need to line up a baby-sitter this weekend, so we can attend the office awards banquet. So I am juggling all these things and all of a sudden I'm getting resentful because . . . you know what? It must be nice to come home and just crash on the couch. But then I go back and rationalize it. Well, you know, he has worked hard today and he does regularly put in seven-day weeks. Yeah, granted I get Saturday and Sunday off. But I'm still working at home and I'm not sitting on the couch on Saturday and Sunday. I'm usually carting this one off to baseball practice and that one off to Brownies. And then I have to figure out how to be in two places simultaneously, because two of the kids' practices are at the same time. During soccer season, all three older children may have practices at the same time at three different fields. So I call the coach or another mom to see who can bring one of the children home. Anyway, I'm juggling all of this at night and on weekends.

You just get in the mode of doing it. I rationalize that these are things that I'm expected to do. Then I just do it. Just get it done. I don't even bring it up for discussion, I just do it. But then it's that one time that Joe will say something like "Why didn't you pick up the cleaning today?" Boy! Then the resentment just pops out. But it passes, and once again I'm rationalizing why I have to do so much.

Tamara and Phil: It couldn't last forever

I really wanted the marriage between Phil and me to work. After all, this was a second marriage for me. So when he turned out to be less responsible than I imagined him to be, I began rationalizing. I just set my jaw and got to work. As a single mom, I had done all the chores *and* worked. So, okay, if Phil wasn't willing to pitch in, I could just continue doing that. While Phil did nothing, I cooked. And cleaned and fed the pets. And shopped. The kids are bigger now, I reasoned. *They* can pitch in more.

But it wasn't easy to be cleaning the bathroom while Phil played tennis with his buddies. Or to be grocery shopping late at night while he watched television. Underneath, I was really resentful. But I didn't say anything. He already had made it clear that he wasn't interested in pitching in. His response was generally "It's all right if the bathroom is dirty. Just leave it." Well, that didn't suit me. I can only stand so much dirt, and the house was already dirtier than I liked. I just didn't have time to keep up with it.

The more I did, however, the less inclination Phil had ever to pitch in. Then, when the same cycle began to occur in our business, the resentment really grew. I worked long hours designing ads and brochures for clients. Phil was working fewer and fewer hours, choosing instead to play racquetball and tennis during office hours.

But I was also resolved to make this marriage work. So I just did more and more. It couldn't last forever, though, and it didn't. Eventually, Phil's irresponsibility was too much. I couldn't cycle through one more round.

The scene was set for a showdown.

Reba and Nathan: Wishalizing

I took rationalizing to a new art form. I always thought that whatever the problem was, it was temporary. I always thought, "I'll get through this."

I thought my early struggles were temporary. I could really identify with the young, single mother in a popular novel who lived in a trailer and couldn't begin to meet all of her two boys' needs, although she obviously loved them. As a young, single mother, I lived on only $415 a month in salary. Peter's medical supplies and therapy were really expensive. But I never felt sorry for myself. I thought that if I worked hard and was a good person who did the right thing, then, at age thirty or thirty-five or forty, everything would smooth out and life would be effortless and easy.

In the meantime, I "wishalized." It was more than just rationalizing. I made things up to suit my story. I fictionalized. At the divorce proceedings with my husband of fifteen years, the lawyer asked us questions and I began to answer. My husband was just looking at me, his mouth wide open.

"I never did that, and I never said that," he said.

As we got deeper into the stories, I realized I had spent fifteen years making things up in my head. Nathan might start a sentence and then I would fill in the blanks to make sense of what otherwise didn't make any. So while he had been spending our money recklessly, I had been filling in blanks with things to excuse it. Things like "He's expecting a big return on his investment next month." Only he never really told me that. I made it up.

"Wishalizing" was my cycle. By making up my own stories, I never had to deal with the reality of the situation, which was that my husband was a speculator with a tenuous hold on reality. I didn't want to see that, so I just carried him and our family and "wishalized" the rest.

Sarah and Marvin: No other option

Even though Marvin and I fought, I felt needed. I rationalized our marriage because I felt significant. Often jobless, always unhappy, Marvin needed me. So, I would hitch up my overalls, so to speak, and keep on trucking. Besides, divorce just seemed like a nonsolution. The marriage was a commitment that had to be fixed, not dissolved.

But the resentment was thick on both sides. I resented having to carry the load. He resented my strength. His resentment came out in two ways. First, he was unfaithful. Second, he often put me down in public. My friends didn't know about the unfaithfulness. But they knew about the verbal abuse.

"Sarah, why do you allow him to do that?" one of my friends asked me after Marvin directed a particularly virulent attack at me during dinner. "You are such a strong person, but around Marvin you get quiet and say nothing when he says these stupid, ugly things about you."

I didn't know what to say. But it was because I felt responsible for him, and divorce simply wasn't an option.

Kate and family: Reducing my stress

I was the problem solver in my family, ready with help for any circumstance. I ran around like an ant picking up the debris of others.

One particular area in which I helped was balancing checkbooks for my mother and two of my elderly aunts. What a disaster! Seldom were the check amounts recorded right, if they were recorded at all. Double entries on the deposits were always fun, and bank drafts for mortgage and insurance payments seemed to be invisible to them. I experienced the same kinds of problems with their Medicare reimbursements, insurance . . . the list went on and on.

I rationalized that they must be incapable of doing any of this for themselves, and that I was the only one in the family who understood all these important details. I needed to help them, but it was taking too much time and added to my frustration level. How could I reduce the stress this was causing in my life?

The answer seemed obvious. I would just do it all for them from the beginning rather than let them do it and then clean up the mess. So I added my name to their bank accounts and had the bank statements come directly to me. One step saved. Then they brought me their bills and I would write the checks and mail them. This took a little extra time, but by having it done right, reconciling with the bank statement was a snap. Presto. Less stress. At least at first.

As my load grew heavier, I started getting behind on getting the bills paid and mailed. My resentment grew, but I kept doing it, thinking that they couldn't do it without me. So the cycle kept spinning.

Friends and the Four R's
Reba and Jenny: Date and steak

Jenny and I have been friends forever, it seems, but I have spent half of that time being exasperated with her. I never could understand why she didn't pull her own weight. This is a small example, but it is typical of our friendship.

While we were in college and on such a tight budget, we had a deal. Any time one of us was asked on a date, we'd order a steak and eat only half. We'd bring the other half home, and then we would all have steak and eggs for breakfast. Well, I was always the one to bring steak home. Jenny almost never went out on a date.

I became quite exasperated and *resentful*.

"This is not fair," I said. "Why don't you go out and get a date for a change?"

I don't know why I thought she would. This was the same friend who wouldn't get up in the morning to keep her job. Why would I think she'd bring steak home? But I'd think about how much she needed me, and the cycle continued.

Joan and Helen: The friendship ends

My carrying Helen ended a friendship, but I never saw it coming, really. I mean, I had done so much to help, I thought. I had handed her a new career. I gave her a place to live while she supported her husband's art career. I adopted her into our family.

I thought I was helping, but what I was really doing was stripping her of her confidence and self-esteem. I put her in a place where she was very uncomfortable. And I did it all in the name of love.

I was constantly trying to help her and show her how to do the work. I'd take on new clients and then try to walk her through how to handle the account. But she was living in my shadow, really. I was out rowing as hard as I could row to get more business, business I really shouldn't have even taken on, to have enough money for Helen, too.

Finally, I began to notice that our relationship was changing. I had routinely asked her to accompany my best friend and me to lunch or to an event. Now, when I asked her to go places with us, she would turn me down, saying she wasn't interested. She would make little snide comments about what was happening with various clients.

I basically knew she was resentful about something, but I ignored the signs. It was as if she had fallen from the boat, but I was so busy rowing up front, I couldn't turn my head to see I was losing my passenger.

Finally, one day she faxed a bio to the office for our administrative assistant to type. On it, she was claiming credit for all my clients. The administrative assistant called and said, "Joan, I need to talk to you." She told me about the bio, and she also cautioned me that there was something wrong with Helen. I was working three major projects and I was too busy to think about it. "Thanks," I told my assistant. "I'll talk to her when I can get some time."

Getting time took about two months. By then, Helen was really resentful. We could barely speak cordially. She accused me of being arrogant, in thinking that I had special skills. She was thinking of going out on her own, using the contract formulation, the media plans, the strategies I had developed over a period of time, and taking those clients I had recruited and given her to handle.

Well, that conversation ended a twenty-year friendship. What happened in retrospect is that in carrying her, I caused her to begin to resent me and her growing dependence upon me. It was a big lesson for me.

Work and the Four R's
Michelle: Keep the machines going

I started doing more than my job, plus others, for two reasons. I wanted to help, and I had adopted the mother-hen role early on. But another major reason was the line of work we did. We supplied parts for medical equipment. I understood like no one else how important it is that all the parts on a piece of medical equipment work. If the dialysis machine I needed was down for lack of parts, where would I be? I knew that if a part wasn't sent out, someone out there might be deprived of medical services. So, if an equipment part for an X-ray machine was requested, I would bust my butt and make sure it got out on the next flight, even if everyone else had gone home. I would push myself.

And so everyone asked me to do extra stuff. "Oh, Michelle, would you do this?" They were nice and said thank you, but they knew if they asked for something, I would do it.

But the resentment did creep in, as the exhaustion set in. I remember once telling my boss, "I am supposed to be here as a handicapped person, and I'm doing more than any of the normal people in this office."

But those hospitals were depending on me, so the cycle continued.

And so the cycle continues until some event or series of events happens to shock us into change.

Your Story

What cycles of carrying are you caught in:

- At home?
- With friends?
- With family?
- At work?

Chapter 6
When the Cycle Stops: Turning Points

Carrying often ends when we are exhausted, worn out. We are burned out, broken down to where we can carry no more. The illusion that we can control events and people outside of ourselves inevitably shatters. We call that a turning point, a point at which we can never return to our old ways.

Occasionally, life hits us with a thunderclap so loud we awake from our illusion and jump to our feet instantly, ready to move. Only in retrospect do we realize the blessing of these devastating experiences. They compel us to make smart choices.

For me, it was a $300 phone call.

I was in South Africa, teaching a roomful of Afrikaner corporate executives how to relate to people of color. It was a tough assignment. And I was alone in a strange country with no friends close at hand. It gave me plenty of time to think. I pondered my growing business, the increasing gap between my husband and me caused by that business, his increasing reliance on me to take charge of everything, and my willingness to do it.

And not only my husband relied on me. I was, by this point, a successful alumna of my tiny rural Arkansas high school and a bit of a celebrity in my family's farming community. My family was now calling on me when they needed help. So were old friends and neighbors.

One night, I woke up at 3 A.M. at my wits' end and called my husband. And I just started to cry. I don't cry often, but this was a real torrent—the kind of crying where you are sobbing from deep in your gut, and the words come out in gasps between sobs.

"Everybody calls me," I sobbed, "my family, my friends. But who am I supposed to call? I'm supposed to call you, but you aren't there anymore."

My accountant husband was quiet through all my sobbing, interjecting an occasional "Hmmmm" in response. At the time, I blamed him for not responding with equal emotion. I mean, I was falling apart.

In retrospect, though, I realize I had as much to do with our situation as he did. I built this package myself from scratch, and I didn't like it, and it hurt from the inside out. Our marriage didn't end at that point. We shared religious values that made commitment a strong bond. But after another few years, we knew we had to separate for both of us to grow. In reality, though, I made that decision in a $300 long-distance sobfest from a South African hotel room. That was my turning point.

Each of the women in this book had a turning point, a single event or series of events, to which she could point when it seemed as if she had been hit on the head with a two-by-four. The "two-by-four experience" slammed each woman so hard that she could no longer hide from the choices she had made that brought her to that point.

Sarah: The last straws

I had two turning points, one at work and one in my marriage. Interestingly, they occurred within the same year.

The two-by-four in my marriage hit shortly before our twenty-fifth wedding anniversary. Our daughter, Diane, was grown, Marvin was unemployed, and I was growing increasingly independent. I was going on a trip with a girlfriend. We'd been planning it for months, and I was pumped. One week before I was to leave, I got a phone call. Actually, I had seven phone calls—messages stacked up on our answering machine when I arrived home. Marvin was calling from jail.

Someone had cut him off while he was driving. At the stoplight, Marvin jumped out of his car, rushed up to the car that had cut him off, opened the door, grabbed the driver, and hit him full force with his fist.

As I put down the phone, I covered my head with my hands and tried to comprehend. Who was this man? Marvin had been a whiner, a complainer, a quitter. But he was not violent. I was numb. I knew we had reached a turning point. I could go no further.

Several phone calls later, I found an attorney at home who could post the $1,000 bond the next morning. By that time, I was thinking that the man my husband assaulted might well sue us. Should I cancel my trip? I wondered. The next morning as I sat at the jail waiting for Marvin to be released, and trying to comprehend what to me was a surreal experience, I knew I would go on my trip. Nothing Marvin did would impact my life further.

My rescuing days were over.

As we drove home, I told him that I was filing for divorce. I also said I would stay three more months to give him time to find a job. But then I was gone. I don't think he believed me, but I was serious. I left in three months, taking only my car, my clothes, and my computer. He had the house and everything in it we had purchased over twenty-five years. I didn't want to argue over any of it. I just wanted out.

Meanwhile, my office went through a different crisis. As my relationship with Marvin became increasingly strained, I poured myself into work. For years, my real devotion was to career. That's where I got my strokes, my accolades, my sense of accomplishment. I was totally devoted to this company, completely committed.

Then, boom! I was hit on the head with a second two-by-four. It started with a new boss. He decided to change the whole team, but he used me to do it. Although my heart of hearts was screaming at me, "You are being used!," I didn't want to believe that. I chose to believe I was doing my job. Over a period of months, he had me terminate half the sales force. When I hesitated, he'd say things like "Well, you know, you are really a nice person. Perhaps you are not tough enough for this job." He challenged me, and appealed to my competitive spirit. Still, I knew these people were being terminated for the wrong reasons, and being victimized to fulfill his personal ambitions. In the end, he effectively terminated *me* by moving me laterally out of his department. I don't know why I should have been surprised, but it was a hard blow. This company that had given me such opportunity was now treating me and others like throwaway items. I was devastated.

But after I got over the shock, I found the emotional umbilical cord had been cut. I was no longer tied to this company. I actually wrote a letter of resignation. I was going to resign in December, take the vacation time I had coming, and start the new year by job hunting. Then I got a call from the new vice president of human resources.

"Can we go to lunch?" she asked.

"Okay," I said, sure that I was about to be fired.

So I went to lunch, and it was all small talk, getting-to-know-you type of stuff. I'm sitting there thinking, "When is she going to fire me? After dessert?"

Finally, I asked, "What are we here for?"

"I just wanted to get to know you," she said. And she talked about changes she wanted to make in human resources and asked if I would like to join her department.

I told her I was planning to leave, and wouldn't stay unless I was valued and could contribute. That was a breaking point for me. Writing a resignation letter and saying I could leave put me in a new place mentally. After some thought, though, I did take the offer. The new position is working out well. Best of all, I am no longer a workaholic, a carrier at work. When that cord was cut, I discovered a universe of infinite possibilities. I was going exploring.

Michelle: Infidelity and illness break the illusion of control

I could handle anything but unfaithfulness. I went into the marriage with Lionel knowing that he was a part-time worker. He held construction jobs when he needed to, but his heart was in his music. As the lead singer in the band, he naturally attracted women, but I trusted him on this issue. For one thing, he always introduced me to the crowd, pointing me out as his wife.

But I couldn't make every gig the band played. Between my dialysis treatments and my job commitments, I missed quite a few.

About five years ago, I noticed Lionel was not as affectionate. He would come home in the evenings and go straight into the bedroom to change and wash his face. No hugs and kisses at the door. I had an ugly premonition.

One afternoon, I dropped by my mother-in-law's home. She was sitting outside at a picnic table conversing with a woman. When they saw me, the woman got up quickly, grabbed two small children, and left before I could come over and say hello. I had seen this woman before at Lionel's gigs. When I asked my mother-in-law who she was, my mother-in-law simply said she was a neighbor. But I could tell she was lying from the way she said it.

Not long after, I asked Lionel if he was having an affair. He got up angrily without answering and left the room. Later, I found out he had gone into the living room. He was sitting in the dark crying because he didn't know how to answer me.

He *was* having an affair. I found out later from friends he was seeing that woman with two kids, a welfare mom with no job and little prospect of one. Not long after, he came home and told me what I really didn't want to hear. "I'm not happy," he said. "I'm leaving."

I found myself sitting on the floor, crying hard, and asking, "What did I do? What did I do to deserve this?"

That was one of the turning points in the carrying cycle. When he left, I picked myself up, and thought to myself, "Michelle, you came to peace about being alone a long time ago, long before Lionel came into your life. You have a job. You have your church. You have your faith. You can return to that life. It's a good life." Within just twenty-four hours, I was set to go forward without him. Or so I thought. But the pretense of thinking I could do it all with just a snap of the fingers was coming to a close.

Lionel not only asked for forgiveness, but he actually sought out a marriage counselor. He came back willing to make a new start. I took him back. The romantic side of our relationship was restored. Lionel really courted me. I felt like a beautiful young woman again. Lionel never admitted he had had an affair. But, in some ways, he showed me he had changed. He gave up the band. He worked a forty-hour week at a company. He was home at night to talk to me. He often took me to my dialysis treatments. We were more honest about our expectations with one another. Still, I kept a close watch. Not all doubt was erased.

And I was still carrying the financial responsibilities. I was still "strong Michelle." And I began to think that every day since 1975, my whole world had been work, dialysis, work, dialysis, work, dialysis. I felt tired. Very, very tired.

Suddenly, my long-held expectations that I could be strong

under any circumstance disappeared. My two-by-four didn't just swat me. It pounded me into pulp. I broke down. I wasn't strong. I was weak. One day at work, I cried and couldn't stop. My boss sent me home, and I called my doctor and told him I needed help.

"Michelle, you have always been strong," he said. "I use you as a role model for every dialysis patient I've ever had."

But I wasn't a good role model anymore. I felt as if I had been pretending to be strong for twenty years and I could pretend no more. I called my sister, and she told me the same thing.

"Michelle, you are always strong," she said.

I told my brother I probably wouldn't see him again, but he didn't believe me, either. So I put my little mask back on and went back to work. But I broke down again. Something was really wrong. In retrospect, I know now I had a nervous breakdown.

I decided to quit work and go on disability, a course I had never taken, although I was eligible. Suddenly at home alone after years and years of working, I found myself with time to think. I felt as if I had spent a lifetime pretending everything was normal when it wasn't. It was a big cover-up. I had pretended I could take care of myself, others, my family, my husband. Now, I felt as if I couldn't carry myself, much less anyone else.

I had to have surgery on my hand because the dialysis was causing so much pain. After the surgery I sat on the couch, and made a decision. No more dialysis, I thought. No more pain, I decided. No more husband. No more bills. No more nothing. I am just going to sit here until I die. I was actually happy about this decision. When I missed dialysis, my husband asked me what was wrong, and I told him about my decision.

"This isn't about you," I explained. "It's not about anything you have done. I just can't cope anymore. I have done everything for everybody. But now I'm dead. I feel like a shell."

My aunt came, and then my sister. They took me to the hospital, a lifeless lump.

I just lay in my bed. I wouldn't go to counseling. They gave me medication but it didn't help.

"What's the use?" I thought.

I wouldn't join in. Then came my real two-by-four. A young woman, in her early twenties, came to see me. She sat on my bed. She had Hodgkin's disease and sickle-cell anemia. She was at the clinic in her last days of life. She was living one day at a time.

"Michelle," she said. "I'm sitting here knowing I'm going to die. And you are trying to take your life. Don't do it."

"But why not?" I asked.

Then she told me about herself. She has a four-year-old daughter whom her sister had recently adopted. She had written her will, and given her sister power of attorney. She even had her casket picked out. But she wanted to live. And I looked at her, and something clicked. Here was a woman who would have given anything to live. How dare I take my life!

I got back into the process. I went to counseling. I had been taking on so much responsibility for so long, and carrying everyone. But the one person I hadn't talked to was me. I didn't know myself. I spent hours walking up and down the hallway, crying. But I was getting to know me.

I finally realized, "Michelle, it *is* you. It was you all the time that made this happen."

I was angry! I was angry at myself. Not at my family. Not at anyone. I had made these choices. It was like I was pretending to enjoy life, but I wasn't really. I was just going through the motions—getting up, getting dressed, going to work, going to dialysis. "Get it over with" was my motto. I lived for Saturday, when I could sleep a little. Then I did it all again.

But I finally realized I did it to myself. I made the choices. The anger kicked in, the tears flowed, and I worked through it. Now, it was time for new choices.

I was going to choose peace, whatever that took. I wasn't going to carry any more. I wasn't going to pretend I could do everything.

Kate: A new life

What began as a turning point in my marriage became a turning point in my life.

The end of my marriage began when Richard came home one evening to tell me that he wanted to move out for six months and think about his life, our marriage, and his future. It was a murky separation, however. At first, Richard didn't move. For the next six months, we lived in limbo in the same house, running parallel but unconnected lives. Finally, I took charge, as usual. Living under the same roof in a pretend state of *life as usual* was just too stressful, especially through the Christmas holidays. I told him if he wanted six months' separation to think about his life and future, then the clock was now ticking. Move.

It took him a month to find an apartment. I would see him when he came to visit our five-year-old daughter, but he said nothing further about his plans. Once again, I took the initiative and asked him what he thought about us as a couple. He was noncommittal.

In the meantime, I began to do well financially with my business, and I became very active in a singles' group at my church. I reconnected with people. And I reconnected with God. As new friends entered my life, I realized that I had withdrawn over my years of marriage because of the fear of having to carry more people. Now, I enjoyed the love and support of others and wanted to keep that in my life.

I even achieved a new love and understanding of Richard, and realized the role I had played in our declining relationship. I had changed. The rules had changed. I wanted to share this new life of love, hope, and laughter with him.

A few more months passed, and Richard appeared at my door. "I think I want to come home," he said.

"Oh? What's different now?" I asked.

Richard explained that he had thought he was really missing something in life by being married, but he had now changed his mind. Being on his own turned out to be tough. He was ready to move back in that night.

My life, however, had changed. I told him that I finally recognized that, in the true definition of the word, we no longer had a real marriage. I shared the new meaning of love I had found through God and new friends. My former self was gone. I wanted a real, loving marriage and suggested that we start marriage counseling immediately to see if we could make it work.

"I need to think about that," he said. Then, he disappeared on me.

I finally called him.

"I took what you said and put it into the formula, and it just didn't work," he finally told me. "I don't think I can live with those new rules."

"That's your choice," I said. "Do you want to file the divorce papers or should I?"

It was too late for us. But it was not too late for me. I was ready to explore a new life.

Reba: Finding debt . . . lots of debt

I am a successful businesswoman, not some naive person. So it is hard to believe that I turned a blind eye to our personal finances. But that is certainly what I did. As stupid as it sounds, I removed myself from any control of our family finances, except for contributing the bulk of the money to the familial pot.

I did it so I wouldn't hurt Nathan's ego. As his fortunes declined and mine increased, I didn't want the difference in our incomes to make a difference in our relationship, so I just handed him the money and never asked about how it was spent. What mattered to me was that Nathan didn't feel like less of a man because of the money situation. I didn't even look at our tax return (although I did know the CPA had prepared it, so I figured it was done correctly). In retrospect I can see how dangerous that was.

Nathan's import-export company was not doing well, actually. Probably because he was always off chasing the next deal, the one that would make him a million. Any money he made he was reinvesting in the company, so I was providing the family support.

My two-by-four came when Nathan was out of town and I answered his phone. A credit card company was on the line, asking for payment. When I asked about the balance, I was shocked to learn it was at the $10,000 limit. The next day another call came in; it was another credit card company, asking about an overdue payment on $15,000 in charges! I was jolted awake!

Where I came from, you never jacked with credit or the checking account. We didn't know anything about sophisticated finance, but we understood that writing a hot check or dumping on your promise to pay was a sin. "Thou shalt not ruin your credit" was the eleventh commandment in my mind. It shook me out of my neurosis about protecting a man's ego. You just don't fool around with my credit rating.

When I confronted my husband, he convinced me that the office computer had screwed up, but he was on the case. He would fix everything. But he couldn't. The creditors were calling. I started to investigate. I had no idea how deep the pit of debt was.

As it turned out, Nathan was an outlaw who broke every rule on money management and family trust. We were gravely in debt. He had forged my signature on five loans. Everything we owned was mortgaged, including my separate property. We had a second mortgage on the house.

When our son's car was repossessed, I was horrified. The severity of the situation was overwhelming. We were staring down a deep hole.

Yet somehow, my husband always felt he was going to make the big score and pay everything back plus lots more. I would never know.

I would have left him right after the discovery of that appalling debt, but he convinced me he might commit suicide. He went into a deep depression. So I just took over the finances and struggled to pay back a staggering debt. Declaring bankruptcy never occurred to me. "Thou shalt not declare bankruptcy" was the twelfth commandment.

It took me seven years to pay back all the debt. But the second two-by-four smashed me three years into the ordeal. My husband was finally feeling better, I guess. I caught him with a twenty-five-year-old redhead. That's when I finally realized I had to make some smart choices for a change. I started by calling a divorce lawyer. I was no longer into protecting Nathan's fragile ego. My husband-carrying days were over.

Joan: Hitting the wall

The realization that I would not duplicate the financial success of my successful businessman father was devastating. For seven years, I poured my heart and soul into forming a business that would grow into an entity larger than myself—I immersed myself in business plans, talked with venture capitalists, set up alliances with major corporations. Now, I was facing downsizing after my expansion partner was sold to another company. Our growth plans died.

Our company would obviously remain a small entrepreneurial venture for the foreseeable future. I had put in long hours. I had done work that I hated, spending hours on accounting issues, writing business forms, conforming to government employment rules and regulations. Many functions that large companies have entire staffs to handle, I handled alone.

And now it seemed that the business was not going to grow, not without access to capital.

For years, I felt I had to be the primary breadwinner. For years, I felt the weight of that responsibility. But I was too exhausted to continue. I felt as if I had been building a pyramid, pushing and pulling each giant stone by myself. I couldn't go get another stone. There was no strength left to push.

I sold the business for a fraction of what we had invested in it. And I went home. I was exhausted, mentally and physically. I had hit the wall.

And my priorities were shifting. I wanted to be home with our daughter. My two older children were in college, and I didn't want to sacrifice my last child to the loneliness of a latch-key existence. Junior high had been the hardest time for my older children, both of whom had often come home to an empty house. I wanted those early teenage years to be easier for this last child.

I decided to take a sabbatical from the business world. Instead, I would work on the book I had wanted to write for several years. And I would be there to take our daughter to soccer practice, volunteer for school field trips, and go over her homework before 9 P.M.

That decision placed my husband and me in new roles. After holding a series of jobs, he had joined our company two years before. When we sold the company, he was also out of work. Nothing in his employment history gave me confidence and trust that he would be able to take up the slack and provide a standard of living that matched our current needs.

But I didn't have a choice. I couldn't carry the load any further. The decision wasn't arbitrary or willful on my part. The exhaustion went so deep, I simply couldn't go forward. I needed time for healing. That was my turning point.

When I first told Allen of my intention to stay home and complete a book project rather than finding full-time employment, he panicked. He was willing to support us, but he didn't have any source of income at that moment, either. He tried a new business unrelated to his former occupation that only threw us more deeply into debt. He decided to go back to his original training. He started a financial communications firm, working out of the house. After a few months, he formed an alliance with a major national competitor. The start was slow, but business has, since then, been steadily growing.

Meanwhile, what started out as one book for me has turned into a book-publishing business, helping others get their books printed and to market.

Between us, our income is returning to its former level.

Tamara: The bankruptcy blues

Bankruptcy was the end of the downward spiral for Phil and me. I was willing to do almost anything to make this second marriage work. I had carried the business for both of us, meeting deadlines and producing advertisements, brochures, and other marketing material for our clients. I had carried the household—shopping, cooking, cleaning, helping the children as best I could with their homework and activities.

But watching Phil desert his responsibilities day by day was too much for me. He slept late, missed deadlines, and missed meetings. From my vantage point, he didn't seem to care at all about what happened to us. He had taken over the finances when we got married, and too late, I realized how deeply in debt we had fallen.

The turning point came when I realized we would lose our home. I had wanted a home for a long time. Now, because of Phil's financial mismanagement, we were behind on payments. And there was no money to make those payments.

I felt totally powerless. I didn't know what to do. I had always made it on my own, and wasn't willing to go down the tubes with him. So I decided I had to separate from Phil.

It took what little courage I had left to ask Phil to leave. I still loved him, but I was also really angry at him. Furious might be a better word for my feelings. After facing the humiliation of bankruptcy in front of all my neighbors, I now had to face the devastation of a failed second marriage. But I could not go on with the marriage as it stood at that low point. I no longer trusted Phil. To survive, I needed to pour all my energies into work and the children. I couldn't carry him, too. Not any longer.

We separated. Phil called every week, but I had so much anger and hurt that I couldn't talk to him. We were apart about eight months. At Christmastime, Phil went to New York to see his dad. Everything was done for the holidays. I was really kind of depressed. The Christmas season felt empty. Susie, my little daughter, came in to my bedroom, and asked if Phil was coming home for Christmas.

"I really wish he could be here," she said.

Something in her voice penetrated the wall I had built. Suddenly, the good memories, all the good times, came flooding back into my consciousness.

"Tell you what," I replied. "I'll call him and see if he wants to come."

He did. He flew in on Christmas Eve, and Christmas Day was a wonderful, wonderful day filled with love and laughter. After lunch, Phil turned to me and said, "I know I've blown it. I want you to know that for the first time I am willing to do whatever it takes to patch things up."

It was a Christmas miracle.

Marta: Workshop wisdom

My two-by-four was a personal-growth workshop that gave all of us attending the freedom to search deep, long, and hard. I was already searching. For about a year I had been grappling with basic issues: Who am I, what am I . . . is it all worth it? It is worth it to keep up with the Joneses? Is it worth it to have a career *and* be a mom? Is it worth it to be a wife, even though my husband works hard and I know where he is 99 percent of the time? (Some of my friends don't know where their husbands are *half* the time.) Still, I wondered, is it worth it?

The six-day workshop gave me time to stop and reflect. It forced each of us to answer soul-searching questions: Are the rules under which we operate valid? Are our preconceived assumptions correct? Is our own world view of how things should be biased by those assumptions?

I found myself questioning everything about my life—how I made my decisions and how valid those decisions were.

In the process, I found a giant hole where the real me was buried. Discovering her was a surprise. But once discovered, I couldn't ignore her any longer. She wasn't willing to go home quietly and do laundry. I finally saw I had choices.

Smart Choices

Whether the two-by-four is a sharp blow, a series of quick hits, a life-threatening experience, or a cushioned prod, it leads the way to radical change. It turns our thinking, and thus our direction, into new avenues, new strategies, new choices.

We generally feel ecstatic after we first begin to make these new choices. What can provide more hope than a new beginning? A new you? We may choose to let go of our controlling behavior and give back responsibilities.

But when a river changes course, it's not during the gentle summer rains. A river changes course at its most turbulent moment, as the floodwaters spill over their banks, carrying debris along the churning currents. We should expect some debris, too. When we change course, it impacts everyone around us. Not all of our friends, coworkers, or family members are going to be happy with our new direction. We need to expect some turbulence and learn how to raft through the churning ripples of others' reactions. That's what we will explore in Part Two: Smart Choices.

Turning Points

These women experienced a variety of turning points that prompted them to action:

- Lack of communication
- Added responsibilities
- Lack of emotional support
- Unfulfilled expectations
- Financial disaster
- Infidelity
- Partner unwilling to renegotiate
- Trust of others weakened or gone
- Unacceptable requirements at work
- Personal insight

Your Story

What turning points have you reached in your relationships at home?

What turning points have you reached in your relationships with friends?

What turning points have you reached in your relationships at work?

PART II
SMART CHOICES

Chapter 7
Choose to Let Loose

Smart women are past blaming others. We know that to go forward, we have to take a look at ourselves and take responsibility for the part we've played in a relationship's imbalance, and make some changes. Control is an issue with all of us who carry.

We keep a tight grip. Loosening that grip is not automatic, nor is it a one-time event. It is a process, and it takes an expanded understanding of when to let loose and why.

Being brought up in the country, I consider the issue of whether I'm carrying on what I call the WINGS Test. It's based on a story from home.

We had a neighbor I'll always remember. Elma was part Indian and loved animals. She had a real rapport with them. One day, her son brought home a nestling they initially thought was a hawk. Henrietta grew into a big American bald eagle. The most common practice in our area with a wild bird, such as a goose, was to clip its wings and make it into a farm pet, because people thought that, once domesticated, a wild bird couldn't function in the wild.

But Elma couldn't bring herself to do that. The eagle lived in a big cage the size of an outhouse that Elma built out of wood and chicken wire. As Henrietta grew, she became so big she couldn't even spread her wings in the cage. One day, against the advice of everyone, Elma took Henrietta out of her cage and set her on the fencepost to let her flap her wings. It was springtime, and all the nesting birds recognized a threat when they saw one. Henrietta was swarmed by blue jays and mockingbirds, which often dive-bomb potential predators. She was ducking and dodging. Then all of a sudden, she took off. She was one surprised bird! She didn't know she could fly.

About two hours later, a neighbor called Elma and told her Henrietta was on her roof and wouldn't budge. Elma took a ladder and climbed up on the roof to get her. The desperate eagle climbed on Elma's shoulder and stayed there, as Elma climbed down and walked back to her home. It was quite a sight.

Henrietta probably didn't want to leave that cage again. She had been truly frightened. But after nesting season, Elma again put her out. This time, Henrietta took off. We never saw her again. Elma understood that a wild bird needs to be wild to be happy. She gave that eagle her wings.

We have to be willing to do the same. We have to teach those around us to fly, rather than us clipping their wings and doing it all. This means we have to give up control, to let loose, to give others their wings.

WINGS is an acronym for questions we need to ask ourselves before we jump in "to fix" the situation for others.

W stands for Wanted	Is our help wanted? Did the person ask us for help, or are we imposing our "help" because we think something needs to be taken care of?

I stands for Investment	Is this action an investment in the person's potential, or simply wasted effort?
N stands for Nurture	Does our involvement nurture the person's self-worth, or rob the individual of choice?
G stands for Growth	Does this action promote the person's personal growth, or does it allow the individual to avoid responsibility?
S stands for Soar	Does our involvement encourage the person to soar to new territory, or does it trap the individual in the same spot?

Giving up control means allowing others to do things differently than we do. It may mean allowing them to fail. It requires us to be more flexible on lots of issues, such as time frames, methodology, sequence, and standards. We have to learn where we can compromise and accept the differences between us and others.

And realizing we need to change is only the first step. Achieving change is like riding a seesaw. While we may make significant changes at first, we may also find ourselves regressing into old behavior in an emergency, or when we meet resistance from others. That is to be expected. And it is okay. But we need to be prepared for reactions in ourselves and others. Expecting reactions will soften the element of surprise.

Reactions from others can be positive or negative. At worst, we find that while we are making new choices, others in our life are unwilling to do so. That is why some women who make new choices may end up in divorce court. But just as often, the women's partners may be willing to make new choices also, placing their marriages on a strong and forward path.

Reactions, positive and negative, happen at all levels. Your coworkers may react positively to your new choices. They may react negatively. The same is true of family members. Be prepared. When you change, others react. We can't expect instant gratitude when we hand responsibility back to others. Our coworkers or family members may appear shocked and angry, and we can expect resistance as the balance of responsibility adjusts between us. Others may not reassume responsibility. We have to just lay down that ball and walk away. In some cases, a person may leave your life once the balance changes.

You may experience different emotions as you pass through change—anger, guilt, discouragement, fear. You must have the confidence in your heart that you are doing the right thing for your coworkers and family as well as for yourself. It takes that confidence to stand firm. Otherwise, retreat is common.

Timmy and Patty provide a classic example of a negative reaction to change. They began as a couple under one set of rules. When Patty made new choices, Timmy reacted with shock and resistance. Patty, caught by surprise and unprepared for his strong reaction, retreated to old behaviors. This is what happened.

I was helping out a friend, acting as mother confessor to her son, Timmy. Timmy and his wife, Patty, had had a huge fight, and my friend asked me if I would go over and see what was going on. My friend had tried to call her daughter-in-law, but the phone was unplugged. The last time she'd talked to Patty, she was in tears.

So I went over. Timmy was there, and I invited him to my house. He came. We sat on the sofa talking and I asked him what was wrong.

"Well, when I met her, when I married her, she used to do everything," he replied. "Now, she wants *me* to do all kinds of stuff."

I couldn't believe my ears! "Why do you think she married you?" I asked. "If she is going to do everything, she might as well have stayed by herself."

We drove to their house, and I sat between the two of them, wondering how I had gotten into this situation again. Before they married, Patty was handling life as a single mom with three small children. She was also nursing her dying father. Her father is now dead, but there is another child, a daughter. The baby is now over a year old and toddling around the house, getting into the usual scrapes of the very young and very innocent.

But Timmy didn't get it. He turned to Patty and said plaintively, "You used to be so strong, and now you want me to help."

"I *was* strong," Patty replied. "I had to be. My dad was sick, and I had three kids to look after. But now I want a partner."

Patty expected her husband to be that partner. But Patty's plea went right over Timmy's head. He wasn't ready to make new choices. He had married a woman who would carry him, and that's all he wanted. He moved out and got his own apartment, using some money he received after his grandmother died.

Patty then relented and took him back under the old rules. She continued doing all the work. This is not an unusual response. It's easy to go back to our old behaviors when the reaction we want isn't what we get. But if Patty really wants her life to change, she will eventually have to institute some of those choices. Perhaps her choices will happen more slowly, one change at a time.

Letting loose happens one decision at a time. For those of us on that road, we have shed some layers of control and have others still to shed. Basically, letting loose happens through three stages. These are:

1. Letting loose of control

This means changing our expectations of ourselves. We must let loose of our perfectionism and our exceedingly high standards for others.

To do that, we must realize that both we and those around us will be happier, healthier human beings when we let loose and give up some control, particularly in those areas in which we try to control others. Our two-by-four experiences often cause the "A-ha!" that starts this mental shifting.

2. Letting loose of responsibilities

We need to give back responsibilities that we have usurped from others. And we may need to shed some additional responsibilities, in some cases hiring others or delegating. Certainly, most of us need to do a better job of sharing joint responsibilities, creating a true team whether it be at home or at work.

3. Letting loose of the choices others make

With the shifting of responsibilities, we need to be prepared to handle the reactions of others. When we change our own behavior, it creates ripples among those with whom we interact, particularly family members and spouses. A change in our behavior also impacts their lives. We change, and they choose how to respond. Their choice may be positive or negative, but it will seldom be neutral.

Letting loose also means letting others learn from their own mistakes. It means letting our growing children spread their wings and fly— a tough hurdle for smart women. It's not easy either to let your spouse do a task in his own way, or let coworkers work out a project, even though you think your way may be better. The outcome, however, may pleasantly surprise you.

All of our women experienced different hurdles and different triumphs in learning to let loose.

Let Loose of Control

Change Expectations of Self

Sarah: I can say no

Before I could do anything about changing my situation, a mental shift had to occur in my thinking. For twenty-five years, I had come from the standpoint that no matter what happened, my marriage to Marvin was cast in stone. Not until my thinking shifted—and I realized that the marriage wasn't working, hadn't been working, and wasn't going to work—

could I make new choices. I had to let loose of the idea that I was committed "until death do us part." It wasn't easy for me to do that. That commitment was part of my identity—I was a wife committed to her marriage.

Once I did that, however, my thinking shifted in other ways. I began to think through all the areas of my life. I changed my priorities. I had taught training courses on setting priorities. I knew what to do. I could talk about the process, but I hadn't done it for myself.

I began by saying "No." My first no was to Marvin. No, I will not carry you any longer. No, I will no longer bail you out of your difficulties. No. No. No.

After my company treated me with disrespect, I was also able to say no when it was appropriate to people at work, and to others. I was often asked to take on extra projects at the office, and to serve on community committees by neighbors. At the urging of some of my close friends, I would sometimes turn down requests, but I also felt guilty about it. I really wanted to help. I wanted to be involved. I felt all this anxiety inside, instead of looking at my schedule and asking myself: Can I realistically do this?

I finally realized that turning down requests was a smart choice, because I had previously made more promises than I could keep. I had a reputation for always being late—late for engagements, and late on projects or other commitments. It was because I was overcommitted and couldn't get everything done. I was always late because I would try to fit in one more task before meeting friends for dinner. Or I would be days behind on projects. After beginning to turn down requests that didn't make sense, boards on which I had no time to participate, projects that I couldn't complete in a realistic time frame, my life really changed.

For the first time, I had time for me—quiet time to let the true me emerge. I began to exercise, to eat better, to spend time with friends, to spend more time with my daughter. I spent less time at work, but my work was not suffering. I did what needed to be done and I did it well. But there is no doubt I could do none of this until I made a mental choice to change, starting with my marriage. It happened naturally. Once I made the mental shift, the other pieces just fell into place.

Once I decided what I wanted, where my priorities were, and what connected me emotionally, then it was easy to move out of my life those things that didn't fit where I was mentally.

Marta: I can do less

Recognizing that I can't do everything was a huge mental shift for me. I never could in the first place, of course. But for a long time I would go through this mental process: What can I do to change this? Then I would make it worse by saying to myself, "Yeah, Marta, you are worthless. You really can't do it all."

This was my emotional reaction to being overcommitted.

Well, realizing that no one, me included, could do it all was the shift. We are all just human, doing what we can. Before, I basically felt I should be able to do everything, no matter how much was on the to-do list. So that shift has helped me with the worthlessness I felt when I let the ball drop.

Recently, we were doing an update at work. But there were a lot of other projects also going on. Basically, I just didn't get around to do-ing my part of the update. When my manager asked for it, I just said, "I dropped the ball on that. I need to move forward on it." That's it. That's all I said. I didn't go into a lot of excuses as to why I hadn't gotten around to it, as I might have done previously.

The next day when I got to work, my manager said, "What can I do to help you?"

I was taken aback. I never asked for help. I always thought I had to do everything by myself. I didn't have an answer. But I thought about it, and came up with several ways others could help get the project completed by tracking down some data. That was a real breakthrough for me. And the project was completed on time.

The interesting side note to this episode came a few days later. An administrative assistant came up to me and said, "Marta, I know I shouldn't have been listening, but I heard the conversation between you and Sue."

"Yeah?" I thought. "Oh, great."

"You were in such control, but not to the point it was intimidating. You were just straightforward and honest and I really think Sue respected that. I think that's great. I wish we could all be more straightforward without being defensive."

Michelle: I can have peace

I had strong signals to let go several times in my life. And I did quit carrying for a while. But I picked it back up.

The first time I quit carrying was when I quit my manager's job because the stress of bearing all the financial responsibility in my marriage was causing my illness to intensify. I ended up in the hospital once too often. So, I just let go and told Lionel to get a real job. I was done carrying.

But I wasn't really. Lionel did get a forty-hour-a-week job, but he was itching to return to his music. As my health improved, I went back to work. Soon, I returned to my old habits. Nothing had really changed in my behavior or thinking. I still thought my sense of worth came from the world of work, and taking care of myself and everyone around me.

Soon I was bringing in enough money to pay the bills. As soon as that happened, Lionel began to play with the band again. Pretty soon, he quit work and was back to music full time. Nothing had really changed.

But after the disappointment of Lionel's affair, and the renewed illness I experienced as I tried to carry all the financial load, I really quit the next time. I quit to the point of not wanting to live. I thought if

I couldn't do all those things I expected of myself, then what was the point?

But at that low ebb, I also dug deep into my soul. The end result was a peace of mind that I had never before experienced as I accepted myself as I am, not as I thought I *should* be. I have really let go this time. And I have never known such serenity.

Kate: I can let go

My journey of change began when Richard and I separated. At that point, I didn't know if *we* had any chance to work together to make changes and save the marriage, but I knew that *I* had a chance for a new beginning, either way it went. I was unhappy with myself and what I had become. In the process of carrying Richard, I also began carrying friends and family, and the quality of my life and relationships suffered.

The first step in letting go was to stop carrying not just Richard but everyone, including friends and family. Easier said than done. I didn't have the power to do it alone. I began with a prayer of forgiveness for them and myself and gave it all to God. I had always believed in God, but had never put him in control. Boy, that was tough, giving up control. But when I loosened my grasp, the burden lifted, and new people and opportunities entered my life.

The first visible sign of the new me was letting loose of worry. Worry about my future and the millions of things I always had to do contaminated everything I did. When I was playing with my daughter, Joy, I worried about the work waiting for me. When I was working, I worried about my homework for graduate school. At school, I felt guilty about time away from my daughter. The internal conflict almost killed me, until I gave my future to God and truly started living in the present moment.

When I spent time with Joy, I gave her my full attention. I began to see the world through her eyes. She saw a world of simple pleasures and lots of laughter, and I began to laugh with her.

I let go of the worry about financial security. I discovered that money was there when I needed it. When I decided to go to graduate school, my work was slow, so I volunteered to help a young pastor start an inner-city mission church. I had money in savings from my car-wreck settlement, so I wasn't worried. But over the next few months almost no work came in. So I just gave my extra time to the mission. As the months went by and my savings disappeared, my family began to pressure me to "get a real job" and not go to school. But I was not worried. I had a profound trust that I was doing what I was supposed to be doing.

Six weeks before school started, I got a call from a local consultant that I had never met, and he hired me on the spot. I had a contract with his firm for as many or as few hours as I wanted to work for the entire time I was in school.

Change hasn't happened overnight, and new challenges appear often. But just as often, I see miracles in my life that I never saw before, and I thank God.

Joan: I can trust

I carried for ten years. It was by design. But I don't carry any longer. When I burned out, I quit. I had to. Even though I didn't trust Allen to provide a living, I did trust God. Over the past fifteen years, I had been on a spiritual search to better understand God. The first revelation I had was that God is Love, not that God is loving, but that Love surrounds, envelops, and nurtures us completely. Like the air we breathe, Love *is,* and is everywhere.

From this nurturing all-presence, I had only to turn my thoughts to Love to be fed. I began to trust. I had already learned to trust God for my supply as a single mom. I was mightily frightened that I couldn't support my two small children. But I began to understand somewhat that as God provides for the birds and animals, he also provides for us.

I had a graphic demonstration of Divine Love's supply. I was going to school and working part time at a small newspaper. It paid diddly-squat, but provided me experience in my field. The budget was very tight. At one point, I had no money to buy groceries, and wouldn't be paid until the following week. We had some canned goods, macaroni and cheese, and peanut butter, but no perishables. We needed milk, fruit, and bread. We could live off boxes and canned goods, but it wasn't all right with me to not have milk for the children. I remember calling a friend. She said, "God knows what you need before you ask. You just need to trust."

I prayed for that trust and felt better. And I thanked God. What happened next was not a coincidence in my mind. A neighbor came over and said, "We're going out of town. Could I give you the perishables out of my refrigerator? They will go bad otherwise."

We went across the street and she handed me an almost full gallon of milk, fruit, vegetables, bread, even cookies. We had everything we had lacked only moments before.

But that wasn't the end of the bounty. Another neighbor called and said, "We have been to the beach and have all this fresh shrimp. Why don't you and the children come and help us eat it tonight?"

That was a huge lesson for me. We went down and ate this feast of shrimp. We not only received what we needed, but abundance was added to it.

After that I quit tracking every penny. I trusted God to provide, and He did.

I still had to learn to trust more deeply, though.

When I finally let loose of the idea that I, personally, had to provide a basis of wealth for my family and looked to Allen to earn a living, he came through. I believed that God would give Allen answers just as he had me. As for my role, as I prayed, I became more convinced that I needed to be more of a mother to our young daughter, be more available for community and church work. I saw clearly the need for more balance in my life. To do that, I had to be home more.

Before, I was the dominant personality. I set the agenda. But when I asked Allen to step up to the plate and support us, that was a big change. It hasn't been easy for him. He tried a new business unrelated to his former occupation that only threw us into deeper debt. But he was praying, too. He decided to go back to his original training. He started a financial communications firm, working out of the house. After a few months, he formed an alliance with a major national competitor. The start was slow, but business grew steadily.

And as I regained my natural energy, I began to work full time once more, only out of our home this time, so my schedule was more flexible. I could be home when our daughter got home from school. So Allen and I now were sharing the financial responsibilities. But we really were equal partners this time. I wasn't carrying more than my share. Letting loose had taken off the pressure.

Let Loose of Responsibilities

Give Responsibility Back

Tamara: You're on your own, kids

I remember a big shift in my thinking about the children when they were small. Every morning we would go through a routine of looking for shoes, or homework, or some other item. I ran around for ten or fifteen minutes helping to locate shoes, coats, and other stuff. Finally, one morning I realized that this routine was the reason I left the house every morning with my stomach in knots. I decided to stop this cycle.

I called a family powwow. I told the children that since I had not worn their shoes, I couldn't possibly know where they had left them, or their jackets. From now on, I wasn't going to hunt for anything. And I didn't.

It took a few mornings, and we were really late the first morning as the kids whined and cried that they couldn't find whatever they were looking for. I just sat in the living room and watched "Good Morning, America." I didn't lift a finger. I finally announced the car was leaving. When we left, my son went without his jacket and my daughter had on old tennis shoes.

They quickly improved. Before many mornings, they adjusted. My daughters began to get their stuff together at night. My son never got that far, but he didn't ask for help anymore as he hunted, either. And he learned to find his stuff pretty quickly. Otherwise, he faced the wrath of his sisters, who didn't want to be late.

Sarah: Not on my credit card

I spent a lifetime taking care of every little detail for my family. It's hard to break that pattern. But I am choosing to do so now. The other day my daughter Diane called. She wanted to rent a car, but her credit card was maxed out and the rental company said no. She was calling to "borrow" my credit card. My instinct was to help. But my new shift in thinking said, Wait a minute. Don't do the same things you did with her father. If she starts calling you now to bail her out and you do, then it's going to be a pattern, that old cycle of carrying.

So I said no. She was surprised, and afterwards, I explained why. She got the message, but she was also a bit angry. I believe that now I'll be the last person she calls. She will have to be really down and out before she risks hearing no again. Also, I hope she understands that it is important for her to make it on her own as a twenty-five-year-old woman.

Kate: No without guilt

A big mental shift came for me when I learned the difference between caring and carrying. When I understood that carrying someone does not help them, I quit feeling guilty when I said no. And the opportunity to say no came often.

My cousin, John, graduated from college recently and his mother asked me to help him get a job. I didn't jump in so fast this time.

I told her, "If he sends me his résumé, I would be willing to give him the numbers of people that might be interested in interviewing him."

I made it clear that I was not going to call him and pressure him to do anything.

The old me would have called John and demanded that he send me a résumé. Time was wasting. If I hadn't made that attempt, I would have felt guilty, as if I hadn't done everything I could to help.

This time, I just let John make his choice without any pressure from me. If he wanted to look for a job, that was fine. If he didn't, that was fine. It was his life. I cared about him, but I was not going to cross that line into carrying. He never called, but he did finally find a job.

Then I had another opportunity to practice my newfound resolve not to carry. John asked if I would loan him a thousand dollars to move into a nicer apartment. I had loaned him money in the past. I guess I should say gave him money. But I feel differently now. It's not my job to make sure his living arrangements are at a certain standard. He has to make his own decisions. I told him no. He tried to blame me for being stuck living in a place that wasn't up to his expectations. At one point, I would have taken on that guilt. Not now.

He needs to make his own choices about where he works and how that impacts where he lives. He needs to farm his own land. That's a big shift for me.

Tamara: Splitting the list

I didn't know how Phil would react when I chose separation. I just knew I wasn't willing to continue without changes on his part. At one level, the choice was very freeing for me. I was not destroyed, by any means. I moved into a small rental house and concentrated on building a graphic arts business and taking care of our family. I felt I was on an upward trajectory again.

Evidently, my choice acted as a catalyst for Phil. I guess he felt safe enough before we separated to give his funk full rein. Our marriage provided a cocoon. Or perhaps he felt he couldn't do what he really wanted, and that was causing his depression. I don't know. But I know my leaving shocked him. He didn't really think I would do it.

But when I left, he really began to take action again. He enrolled in a master's program for creative writing. He began to regain control of his life.

After we reunited, I recognized I could live with him only if he made changes. I didn't want to continue being angry, because I was carrying too much of the load. And he changed. He really did.

Now we are partners. After we really started talking, and Phil was listening, we made a list of everything that needed to be done every week, and split the list down the middle. Phil never believed all those chores were necessary, but he was willing to do them based on my strong feelings about the need to clean up our home. I let him pick which chores he most wanted to do. I took the rest.

Now, Phil's hands-on experience has revolutionized his attitude and his behavior. He understands how much energy it takes to keep a house going, and he has assumed more responsibility for doing chores.

Phil is also back to taking very active, visible roles in the community. He has instituted a writers' program and brought best-selling authors to our small-town library. Everyone was surprised we could get such talent here. He's really a self-starter now. And he's on community boards again, bringing fresh, creative ideas to the organizations. He's done a lot for this community and for us. Dividing up the responsibilities was a gift to us both.

Joan: Yours, mine, and ours

Letting loose of financial control meant sharing on all fronts, including decisions. The wonderful aspect of that choice is that my relationship with Allen is a thousand percent better.

One interesting reaction is that Allen is no longer so passive. When he disagrees, he says so. We fight sometimes. That's all right. I can handle a few good fights. It clears the air. I don't hang on to stuff. Now I know what he thinks and, after I've had a chance to think about it myself, I often agree with him, or we change the situation to accommodate both our views. We are finding true solutions, rather than simply letting Allen resist passively by not doing something.

Now, we understand much better what each of us is willing to do. And it's working much better. Because we are both self-employed, our responsibilities change quite a bit depending on what we are handling at work. Last year, Allen had a huge project and was working very long hours. Since I had a smaller load, I did all the carpooling for Angela, the grocery shopping, and most of the home chores.

This year, however, I am working on a project that is taking all of my time, plus a little more. Allen's time is more flexible right now, and he is doing the carpooling. There are times when we are both busy, and our home life will change again. We'll eat out every night. We'll have to make arrangements for someone else to cart our daughter around, or we'll take turns. But whatever the decision, it involves both of us. That has placed us on equal footing.

Tamara: Finding financial solutions

After Phil and I got back together, we also found financial solutions. I learned two valuable lessons at this time—the value of bringing in an independent third party, and accepting help rather than insisting on doing everything myself.

Phil finished his master's degree in creative writing and became a teacher. It still took both our incomes barely to make ends meet. We met with a financial planner, a personal friend. Bringing in a third party and developing a plan together gave Phil ownership in the budget. I was not forcing it on him.

Our friend offered us her help for free. At one time, I might have insisted on paying. Now, I just accepted the service in the spirit of giving in which it was offered. After years of thinking I had to do everything by myself, it felt wonderful when someone offered help and I accepted. It was completely a gift. She genuinely wanted to do that for us. I felt so loved.

Our friend started us on the plan she had adopted for herself. She had developed it from a lot of ideas she gleaned from others in her field. Our finances were totally out of whack. I always felt like we didn't have what we needed. We were always lacking something. We had college debts, medical debts, credit card debts.

We now have a plan first to pay off school debts from the children's college expenses, then to pay off our mortgage, and, third, to set aside funds for retirement. Keeping to this plan requires a budgetary discipline that Phil has never exercised before. We don't eat out. We rent videos rather than going to first-run movies. We shop for bargains. We don't use credit.

When our dishwasher broke, the cost of a new one was not in the budget. At first, we washed dishes by hand, but after a month we decided there must be a better answer. An appliance store was offering new appliances on a zero down payment basis, with no payments due for a year. We bought one. Over the year, I sent in every rebate I could find from our purchases. By the time the first payment on the dishwasher was due, I had saved $487, the amount it took to pay off the dishwasher.

We are making great progress. Our debts will soon be paid. I actually feel a sense of abundance. I spent most of my adult life feeling poor and stretched out financially. It's a wonderful change.

Sarah: Practicing teamwork

At work, we were preparing to do a brainstorming session about procedures and structures at the office that might need changing. Of course, I wanted to make sure we got everyone's contribution. It was great.

I said, "Okay, now that we have everyone's input, let's prioritize and go back through the list and start coming up with solutions and new procedures."

Before we got in very deep, one of the staff members said, "Sarah, before we get too far into this, do you have a vision or a plan for accomplishing the changes?"

And I thought to myself, "Oh God, am I exposed or what?"

What they were saying to me was they didn't want to waste a whole day going through this exercise if I already had it figured out. That was a real eye-opener for me. I don't tell people, "This is the way we are going to do it." I never have been one to go out and slam-dunk anyone. I draw people in and listen to their ideas, but then I counter with my own. My ideas are good, to be frank, and pretty soon, everyone is agreeing with my ideas. So now they were asking to be let out of the process, and not because I wouldn't listen to them. Rather, they were saying, "Why don't we get Sarah's ideas first and then just add to that?"

I realized I must include them in the idea process without having a second agenda. Before, even though I was listening, I still knew what I wanted, and I was eventually going to sell them *my* ideas. I knew where the process was going to end.

With that realization came the understanding that I wasn't letting people grow. They needed to stretch and make some mistakes. That's how we all learn. That's how I learned in the first place. I wasn't doing my staff a favor by coming in with my own plan. So, I let loose that day and truly let them prioritize without my input. Then, I let them come up with solutions. I kept my mouth shut. That was hard, believe me.

The surprise for me was that they came up with one solution I hadn't considered, and it was very innovative. We are going to implement it. If it doesn't work, so what? We will choose a second solution.

Let Loose of Choices Others Make
Prepare for Ripples and Reactions
Michelle: Shocked by accusations

At one point, I was struggling with illness. I needed some time. I went to my boss, and he maneuvered a paid week off. When I returned, the place was in shambles. My desk was piled high with expense reports and other forms the salespeople didn't complete. They were used to my doing it. Also, I drew most of the customer-service calls, and several problems were festering on the service side when I returned.

I was shocked at how some had reacted in my absence. Two of the guys wrote me up, saying I had caused mistakes that I hadn't. *They* had made the mistakes. I wrote an addendum to the report telling my side, but my outlook changed. I felt betrayed. I had bailed out these two guys so many times. I became kind of snappy. If they asked me to help, I would tell them I was too busy and to do it themselves. I stood my ground.

When I became really sick a few weeks later, I had to take off again, this time for four weeks. After the last experience, my manager took a new tack. He hired two temps to do my job. He also must have talked to the staff, because they were trying to do more by themselves.

They were supposed to be doing these tasks all along, according to their job descriptions, but because I had picked them up, some of the salespeople hadn't bothered to learn.

When I returned, my manager asked me to stage some seminars and training sessions to teach the staff how to handle customer service better, and how to fill out various forms. He finally realized the staff didn't know a lot. They were just kind of getting by, you know, like in school when you didn't know your ABCs but got someone else to push you through. When my manager realized that, he took positive steps to retrain the staff. I was delighted.

Joan: Hurt by ingratitude

I really blew my friendship with Helen. I was shocked at her ingratitude for all I had done to establish her in a new career. When she took credit for my work to establish her own firm, I felt betrayed. I couldn't understand why she was so resentful and angry with me. As a Monday-morning quarterback, I would do it differently. Hopefully, I will next time I am presented with a similar situation.

I thought I was helping Helen, but I can see that asking her to follow my lead was a mistake. I should have been her friend, but let her work out her own solutions.

Since Helen left our company, she has returned to work as a financial manager. Without my interference and trying to fix everything, she might have done that in the first place.

I'm trying now to repair the friendship. We attend the same church, so I see her every Sunday. We are cordial, but not confidants by any means. I hope we can be again someday. She is still carrying her artist husband. It will be interesting to watch what happens in her life. But I'm certainly not going to interfere again.

Sarah: Accepting what is

When I finally shifted my priorities from work to a more balanced perspective, I got a big surprise. I was now ready to spend lots of time with my grown daughter. But she wasn't nearly so ready to spend time with me. Diane had her own life and her own interests.

"We never did all this family stuff before," she told me one day when I asked if she wanted to go shopping with me. "Why all of a sudden do we need to do this?"

At first, I was devastated. Sarah, I thought, you have really screwed up. Why didn't you get this message earlier? Why didn't you spend more time with Diane while she was still at home?

But I worked beyond that feeling. I had to realize that my dream of renewed family time wasn't going to work the way I had envisioned. Diane is spending more time with me, but I know it will never be as much as I would now like. I can't expect her to shift her priorities to fit mine. I have to realize that is okay, too.

Reba: Loving tough

At one point, our oldest daughter, Darlene, at the age of twenty-six, was living at home and struggling to get on her feet. I struggled with how much to carry versus how hard to push. We reached a turning point with the phone bill. We agreed she could live at home rent-free for a while and work off her college debts. But she was supposed to pay for her other expenses. One of those expenses was her share of the long-distance phone bill.

Well, two months came and went, and she hadn't paid her phone bill. Part of me wanted to ignore it, because I knew that some car repairs and other unexpected expenses had set her back on her debt-repayment plan. I did ignore it for two months.

Finally, as the third month approached, I realized I had to take action or I would again be carrying her beyond a point of helpfulness. I realized I would be setting her up to sponge off me for a long time to come. I asked her about the bill. She mumbled something about paying, but a week went by, then another, and the bill wasn't paid. I debated what to do. Then, a new bill came in. Her charges were more than ours.

I took a new approach. I wrote a formal letter, demanded payment, enclosed copies of the unpaid bills, and signed the letter with my full name rather than as "Mom." Within two hours after her arrival home that evening, I found a check on my desk for the full amount. She didn't leave a note. She didn't say a word. I know her well enough to know she was somewhat angry. But within a day the anger was gone. That was the last of the unpaid expenses. From then on, she understood that she was to meet the financial obligations upon which we had originally agreed.

As a family, we were still carrying her, but we had maintained our chosen limits of what that carrying would include. That was a small victory.

Marta: I'm not alone

I had a real tendency to layer on responsibilities at work. The incident in which I didn't get my update done on time and solicited help at my boss's suggestion led me to consider working with partners rather than doing everything all by myself.

Recently at work we were in a very reactive, rather than proactive, mode, which doesn't allow you the opportunity to really think situations through strategically. Thus, the situation may not come out the way you would have liked. That just goes with the environment sometimes.

But I was being asked to take on a new area dealing with disabilities, and I hadn't been able to give it much time or attention. So, I approached my manager and asked her what we might do to free up some time for me to tackle this new area. We talked about what I could get off my plate. As usual, my tendency was to say, "Nothing." I didn't want to let go. It was another one of those "I can't keep the house clean, but I still don't want to let loose" scenarios. If I don't do it myself, I felt, it won't be done right. Or I'd feel a sense of failure: I *should* do this.

I sat there and said, "Okay, Marta, this is your chance to think and choose differently. What can you truly let go of that isn't critical?" There is always something that no one will notice if it doesn't get done, like the dusting at home.

I moved a few items off my list. Of course, the next day, my voice mail was still full, and my manager shifted phone calls to me that she didn't have time to handle. So, it's a matter of making the commitment, prioritizing, and still doing those other items that come up every day.

I asked for help. I contacted a couple of people that have been very strong advocates on disabilities within our company and said, "Okay, so how can you help me in figuring out what needs to be done?" They were both delighted to help. Wow! I thought. I don't have to do this all by myself.

I'm building partnerships. I have people to support my efforts by giving me advice and input. I am not alone.

Allow Differences

Reba: Keeping my mouth shut

The hardest, the greatest challenge I've had in personal relationships is to let my children go. I always try to throw my body in front of them and block all harm, fix all problems, smooth all their paths. In other words, I try to prevent them from living life as we in the rest of the world know it. I have found out, though, that people who grow up having everything face a terrible burden. Having everything provided is a terrible block in a person's development. As soon as you need something, there it is.

I did that to my children. I had to recognize a bit late that my mistakes and pain will not automatically be transferred to them. So I have to let them go, and that's a hard deal for me.

One son is in a relationship now with a nice lady, but I know with 100-percent certainty that this relationship won't work. This young woman brings some really big baggage with her. So he will waste the next five years or so attempting to make this relationship work. I have to recognize there is nothing I can do to stop this process. I just hope it's a growth period. Actually, I know he will learn tremendous lessons. Watching him learn is the tough part.

Keeping my mouth shut is another new skill I'm picking up with my children. One of my twin daughters is married to a man I would never choose. He's quite domineering. But he's also a loyal husband and a good father. His controlling attitude would drive me crazy, but it doesn't bother her. They have a wonderful family. I expect they will endure as a couple forever. And she's getting something out of that relationship that is obviously invisible to me. So I find it my personal duty to appreciate the attributes he has that are very admirable. And I just stay the hell out of the rest of it.

Joan: Romance in the rain forest

For the first time in our marriage I asked Allen to plan our vacation. He agreed. Then, typical for Allen, he did nothing. For three months, he did nothing. I didn't say a word. I had already decided that I was not going to jump in and take over. That would have been my typical behavior. But I have to admit I was going nuts inside. When is he going to plan this vacation? I wondered. *Is* he going to plan this vacation?

The vacation was in August. We were heading to the Pacific Northwest. In July, I heard Allen begin to make calls. He was planning the vacation! I was elated. It was undoubtedly a very different vacation than I would have put together. Because he called late, Allen couldn't always find accommodations. At one place, we ended up staying in a camping trailer, part of a bed-and-breakfast on the Olympic Peninsula. When

I saw the trailer I was truly surprised. We weren't talking about a big double-wide. This was a little-bitty camper just big enough for a bed and a tiny bath too small for two people to share. By the time Allen called, this was the only accommodation he could find.

But it was a lovely evening. We watched the sun set over the Pacific after having spent the afternoon deep in the recesses of the Olympic rain forest. The camper was parked by a rushing stream, which serenaded us all night. It was one of our most romantic evenings.

The next night we spent at a five-star hotel on Vancouver Island. The juxtaposition of the two evenings made the vacation seem even more romantic. In one we had the luxury of nature. On the other, we enjoyed the luxury of gourmet meals, beautiful rooms, and live music outside our window. I couldn't have planned a more perfect vacation.

I had decided earlier to enjoy whatever might happen because of our different planning styles. I had no idea how much fun it would be to flow with his.

Sarah: Corporate caring

I had a person in my office recently who was going through a really bad time. Jacqueline was very intelligent, very capable and smart. But her recent behavior seemed as if she were trying to sabotage her abilities. She was almost asking to be terminated. And others were ready to do just that.

I called her in and asked her, "What's going on?"

Jacqueline began to unload her troubles. She told me her life was totally out of balance. She was engaged to be married. Her grandmother was sick, and she needed to help care for her. She was traveling four out of five days a week and was tired of it.

"What do you want to do?" I asked.

Jacqueline replied that she wanted to be a consultant and have more flexibility in her schedule. "I need to be in control of my life. I don't feel in control," she said.

"Let me help you," I replied.

She was so shocked and surprised. She had thought she was going to be fired. At one point, she would have been right.

"No, let me help you transition out," I repeated. I wanted to allow her to choose and not be punished for that choice. Jacqueline is going to work part time with us while she starts an independent business. If I can find people that need her skills, I will refer them to her.

Marta: My way, your way, a new way

When I left the workshop on personal growth, I was determined to get household help. Hiring someone was still a big mental hurdle for me. I was the only one of my peers at work who didn't have a housecleaner. I knew this was my own cultural hang-up. I kept telling myself that it was okay to let loose of this responsibility. I wouldn't be tainted for the rest of my life because I couldn't keep my house clean without help. I could, of course, keep cleaning my own house forever. The price would be burnout with a capital B, though.

So, I guess God decided to help. My husband's cousin came to live with us for a while. Selene is in her early twenties. She is now sort of our nanny and household helper.

My big lesson was learning to live with the differences in the way Selene and I kept house. When I came home and found clean and folded laundry stacked on the stairs, I had to bite my tongue. My kids were waiting for me to explode. They knew laundry on the stairs was a pet peeve for me.

But I didn't explode. After dinner, I took Selene aside and thanked her for doing the laundry. Then I explained that laundry or anything on the stairs was a safety issue in our house. If I or someone else was carrying the baby and stepped on laundry on the stairs, we might lose our balance and fall, baby and all. She understood and that practice changed quickly.

On the other hand, I have had to lower my standards in lots of little ways. The bottles in the spice cabinet are now stacked on the shelf any old way. As sick as this might sound, I had them alphabetized, and I liked the order that provided. I could find my spices easily. Now I must hunt every time I need a spice. But I keep my mouth shut. I am allowing more differences than I ever thought I could. I think of the trade-off in terms of having help, and the time it has freed up for me to be with my family or to take care of myself.

Letting loose of control is a freeing experience. Communication also plays a big role in letting loose, as we shall see in Chapter Eight.

Choose to Let Loose

These women found solutions by changing themselves and letting loose in many ways. You can, too:

- Change your expectations of yourself and others
- Seek spiritual strength
- Let go of worry about the future
- Give responsibility back to others
- Share decisions and responsibility
- Fight the urge to overcommit
- Embrace help
- Accept differences
- Allow others to make their own choices
- Stand firm when others react to your changes
- Partner with others at work

Your Story

To whom do you need to give back responsibility:

- In your family?
- Among your friends?
- At work?

With whom do you need to share your responsibilities?

Whom do you need to allow to make their own choices?

What expectations are stopping you from making these changes?

Chapter 8
Choose to Listen

An amazing thing happens to smart women who carry. It affects our ability to listen. We stop listening to ourselves. We stop listening to others. We're too busy, too stressed out to listen, to either the warning signals of our own inner selves or bodies, or to the people around us whom we are often carrying. Yet listening is a big part of the solution.

Through active listening, both to ourselves and others, we can hear the problem in a way that naturally reveals solutions. Active listening means devoting your full attention to what someone is saying. It requires you to listen with a mind that is uncluttered by inner dialogue. We have to hear what the other person is saying, rather than using their speaking time to mentally formulate our own response. Active listening means hearing—stopping the inner noise, distractions, assumptions. All of these are barriers to listening.

We must live in the present moment.

From active listening, we learn to be better communicators. Busy women are not always good communicators. We need to learn to express our feelings and expectations in a positive way. We need to verbalize our needs. We also need to listen to the needs of our spouse and coworkers.

Good communication involves risk. In the beginning, as we make new choices, it may be painful. The risk comes from not knowing the outcome. We cannot control what the other person may do. We are no longer avoiding the issues, sweeping them under our desk and pretending they don't exist. Sometimes when we bring issues to the surface, we don't like the reality we find.

My friend Diana learned a very hard lesson about not listening, not communicating, and avoiding the issues.

Diana was a well-known television anchor in a major eastern city. She had soared above her earliest dreams. But one piece of the dream was missing. Diana, focused on her career, had never married. In fact, she had never even been in love.

At forty years of age, she found a man she thought matched her expectations. On the surface he did. Sam was the CEO of a multinational company. He was an active sixty-three-year-old, nearing retirement, but still handsome, charming, and sophisticated. Sam courted Diana with a passion and ardor unknown in her experience. She fell in love. In Diana's case, love was not blind. It was deaf.

Diana began to hear disquieting things about her beloved. She chose not to hear, however. Listen to her tale, a sad story that ended in divorce within a year of the high-profile marriage.

"About eight months after we had begun dating, Sam proposed. I was thrilled. I had waited forty years for the right man to propose to me. Most men were intimidated by me, by my visibility and income.

"After he proposed and I accepted, he began to tell me about all the bad luck he had had with women. He felt that he had fallen in love with manipulative women who abused him. He told me he never planned to marry again. But now that he had met me, he felt differently.

"Well, I chose not to listen to the message behind this tale of woe. All I chose to hear was the part about loving me. I ignored his other two wives and his five children by five different women. Yep, that's right. Five children by five different women. One by each woman. He was married to two of the women, lived with a third, the other two fell into the frequent-sleepover category.

"The multiplicity of women in his life was a major issue in itself I chose to ignore, rather than address. And there was a deeper issue also. It occurs to me now that I might have questioned why no woman he was involved with had *two* children. This was a major clue about the instability of his relationships. But, again, I chose not to hear.

"The news about our engagement leaked out. The local media made a deal out of it—radio talk-show hosts, the newspaper society column. Sam was furious. Once again, I should have been listening, but I sloughed it off. The media were not unkind, they just treated us as a 'people' item. I just told him it was no big deal. But now I became aware that the whole city knew we were engaged. So that impacted me, too. I really wanted the wedding to go off as planned, so I was not publicly embarrassed.

"That probably impacted my refusal to communicate with Sam on some issues that were beginning to surface. Once, we were in a restaurant and his phone rang. I could tell it was a woman. And I heard Sam tell her he was with his lawyer. I ignored it. I told myself that if Sam didn't want to marry me, he would just say so. I told myself that I shouldn't be thinking negatively, that negative thoughts just showed my own insecurity. I told myself I shouldn't be making assumptions. I had this whole dialogue with myself. I never said a word to Sam.

"Well, I married this fool right on schedule. We had a huge wedding in a big church. The symphony played at our reception. We went on my frequent-flyer miles to an overseas resort.

"No sooner was the honeymoon over than Sam told me he wasn't giving up his own apartment, but planned to rent it. Once again, I didn't like it, but I didn't question it, either. I kept my mouth shut, thinking to myself that I wasn't going to be like those other women in his life. I was going to be a sweet wife.

"Within a month, Sam was staying out all night. I'd page him and in about an hour and a half, I'd get a call back. Sam was an old fart. He was usually asleep by 1 A.M. So, now, where was he sleeping at 5 A.M.?

"By now, I had begun to listen. I heard the voice inside me saying, This man is fooling around on you. I knew I had to confront him. It wasn't easy, because he wasn't willing to engage in a conversation with me. For the first time, I realized I had played right into the hands of a chronically unfaithful man who would not communicate with any woman except at a sexual level.

"Within a few months of our marriage, we were separated. It took another year to finalize the divorce. During this time, I saw a therapist. She told me he was probably addicted to sex, and sex with 'the other woman,' whoever that might be. I was amazed.

"Thinking back, I know he told me all of this. He told me in a thousand little ways. But I chose not to hear. I wasn't listening to my own inner voice, and I wasn't listening to his giveaway signs. I wasn't trying to communicate on a level that would bring all this mess into the open. I chose to be deaf."

The smart choice is to listen. It is a three-step process, as Diana's story makes clear.

1. Listen to ourselves

For many of us, we must change how we talk to ourselves. We need to calm the critic in us, the worrier that nags us constantly, the perfectionist that wants everything right, the victim that ignores bad behavior to keep her commitment and expectations intact.

We also have to listen to our feelings and needs, areas we neglect in our world of increasing responsibilities and commitments. We need to know ourselves.

2. Listen to others

We must overcome the barriers to active listening, ranging from the way we filter information to suit our assumptions to half-listening while we do multiple tasks.

And we must communicate our feelings and needs to others, as well as listen to theirs. We must learn to communicate for meaning.

3. Create safe circles

Safe circles are small, intimate groups of people—formal and ad hoc—who connect with us in life. They provide safety and help through a unity of purpose based on shared values and goals. These circles change over time, and we often need different circles or overlapping circles to cover our different roles. These are our listeners, our sounding boards. In the best of these circles, reciprocity is the rule—we give and we take in a never-ending cycle of mutual support.

Listen to Ourselves

Change How We Talk to Ourselves

Many of us talk to ourselves in ways that keep us carrying. When we learn to recognize these conversations and either silence or refute them, we eliminate one of the voices that tell us to carry.

Joan: Adjourn the committee

How many of us are judge and jury for an idea within ourselves? I can't count how many times I've driven to work playing out a scenario in my mind. I'm playing all the parts. I say . . . then he says . . . then I say . . . then he says . . . By the time I get to my destination, I've role-played the answer to the question without ever asking someone else. Perhaps I've decided that my husband won't take the initiative on an idea. Then I never even present it to him. I decide his response without asking.

I have a friend that calls this process "The Committee." It's as if there is a committee meeting in your head. Before the idea is ever aired, the committee has decided against going forward. I wonder—how many ideas have I killed in committee?

Recognizing the committee is at work is a big step forward. I still find myself playing everyone's roles sometimes, but now I recognize what is happening. When I hear the committee meeting, I make a motion to adjourn. I no longer kill an idea before I actually try it out. It's amazing how many times the roles I've imagined people would take were completely wrong.

Marta: Calm the worrier

I used to imagine the worst-case scenario. My imagination constantly conjured up fantasies of disaster or catastrophe. I was scared of something happening to the children, or finding myself in an embarrassing situation. "What will they think of me if I don't have all these charts completed by tomorrow?" "How can I enjoy an outing with Joe while the children are stuck in front of a television at Grandma's on a Saturday?" "What if I went to San Diego on business and the kids ate fast food for four days? They would all get sick. What a disaster!"

I anticipated the worst and overestimated the odds of something bad or embarrassing happening. My favorite expression was "What if . . ." All of these "what ifs . . ." led me to make herculean efforts to make sure everything was personally accomplished by me. Only by doing it myself could I quiet the worrier.

I'm learning to change that. I went out with Joe to a movie recently even though the worrier was saying I hadn't spent enough time with the kids that week and shouldn't be out at night again. I was pleasantly surprised to find out they were thrilled that Joe and I were finally "going on a date." My girls wanted to help me get dressed and put on makeup to go "out with Daddy." I'm challenging the "what ifs . . ." now.

Sarah: Free the victim

I often felt helpless when I was married to Marvin. My thoughts centered on the concept that "I can't change him no matter what I do. I have to live like this." I was victimized by my own inability to consider divorce.

Marvin was always the victim in his own mind. It was always someone besides himself making his life miserable. His negativity turned on me, and the more I rose up the corporate ladder, the more he berated and put me down. I let him. It was a strange circumstance that I would put up with his verbal abuse, considering my stature at work. But I was resigned (like a victim) to my marriage.

We would meet friends for dinner. Of course, I was late. Everyone, including Marvin, would be there when I arrived. The first words out of Marvin's mouth might be "You didn't let the dog out before you left this morning." Whatever it was, it would be negative. He would put me down all evening, making such statements as "Oh, you don't know . . ."

I continued to play the victim by letting thoughts like "I'll never be able to change this situation" govern my inaction. Now I realize I was stuck only because I *felt* I had no choice.

Kate: Shush the perfectionist

I was always pushing and goading myself to do better. I competed against myself. I was constantly telling myself that my efforts weren't good enough, that I should be working harder, that I should always have everything under control, that I should always be competent. I drove myself harder than anyone I knew. I was intolerant of setbacks or mistakes. My favorite expressions were "I should," "I have to," and "I must."

My perfectionist voice in pursuit of its goals pushed me into stress, exhaustion, and burnout. I ignored warning signals from my body. I often got migraines that incapacitated me. I think it was my body's way of forcing a vacation from the constant pushing.

Now I realize that I can't do everything, and I can't do it all perfectly. And just as importantly, I know that I can find other resources to help me get things done. I never considered this an option before, because I didn't think anyone could meet my standards. But when I started working with others and training them as needed, I developed a precious resource in people who do things differently than I do, but who do a wonderful job.

Now when I hear the perfectionist, I just tell her how happy I am that she's moved out.

Tamara: Silence the critic

My inner voice was always telling me how worthless I was. It was constantly judging and evaluating my behavior. It would point out my flaws and limitations. "I'm not as well educated as my friends because I didn't finish college." "I'm not as smart as others." The critic was always putting me down. It ignored my positive qualities and emphasized my weaknesses and inadequacies. My favorite expressions were "That was stupid!" "Look at how capable So-and-so is." "You could have done better."

The critic made me feel inferior to Phil because he seemed so personable and well liked. I didn't give myself credit for all the work I was doing. I always felt I didn't do enough because I never made it through my whole list of things to do.

I have finally made progress in silencing the critic. When the critic pops up, I counter her. I recount my achievements. Then I can see that I have accomplished a lot—a successful business, competent adult children who love me, good friends, quality work. The critic was never my friend. She promoted low self-esteem. And she promoted guilt. I understand that now.

Learning to love myself was one of my most life-changing experiences.

Listen Inside

We have to acknowledge regularly our feelings and needs—an area in which many of us are pretty rusty. We have been so frazzled, deadline-oriented, rushed, and pressured that it has been years since we thought of ourselves in a kind way. We may have to go back to childhood to remember how to assess our own needs and acknowledge them.

We need to take stock of what is working in our lives and what isn't. To do that, we have to listen to ourselves.

Listening to ourselves heals the illusion that we don't need anything from anyone. In fact, we do need that single rose that says, "Thank you for a nice time" or a job well done. We do need time to be quiet, to exercise, to play, and be creative. We are not the low-maintenance women we pegged ourselves to be.

Marta: The creative me

My epiphany came when I realized at the personal growth workshop that I had to carve out space for me. I had spent the last decade caring for children, climbing the corporate ladder, taking care of the home, participating in the community, being a good daughter to my parents. I wanted to do all these activities, but I suddenly realized I had become lost in the whirlwind of activity I had chosen. I had to choose now to create space for me. I take time every day for that listening. Instead of using lunch to run errands, I write in a journal.

The discoveries I have made through writing this journal have been life-changing. I found a poet inside me that communicates through rhyme. I found a woman with a beautiful soul that I really like. I found a woman with buried creativity that is now bursting with ideas and energy.

Taking time to listen has made me love myself, just as we love a friend with whom we share our innermost feelings. The same phenomenon happened to me. And now I want to make space for this "me" I've discovered to flourish in all areas of her life.

I take time to exercise as I have always known I should. But I never could find time. Now, miraculously, I make time. Often I come home and take a walk. Some days, I use the gym at work, climbing the stair machine or walking on the treadmill.

Miraculous changes have occurred in the short time I've been listening to myself.

Michelle: I want to live

Listen to myself? I had never done that. I had spent the last twenty years determined to live a normal life. I completely blocked out the fact that I had no kidneys and was listed as handicapped on my work form. Living normally to me meant taking care of everyone. In my mind, that's what a woman did—took care of her family, took care of her husband, took care of her friends. It never occurred to me I might also take care of myself, except in the sense of not needing anyone else's help.

After I broke down and became depressed, I finally had to listen to myself. I was in the hospital when it finally dawned on me that I had no right to die from my own self-will. Suicide was not an option. I walked the halls of the hospital in tears, so angry with myself for so much. How did I get to this place? What did I do wrong? I had no doubt it was I who'd placed myself there.

My new friend at the hospital was my salvation. She made me realize how selfish it was to wish for death when she wanted so badly to live. I got quiet and listened.

My mom always told me, "You have to go into the closet sometimes."

I finally realized what she meant. I have to be silent and listen to that inner voice, alone.

I lost God for a while. My healing of spirit came when I found Him again. By quieting all my physical senses and listening, I finally took a hard look at myself, who I am, what I need. It's like now God's my friend, my pal. My buddy. I've been through so much and I could explain it all to Him. Surgery after surgery. Kidney messed up. Liver messed up. Heart messed up. Blindness. Missing the prom, the dating, college. There's no way to explain this to others.

But I am not sad. I want to live. Through my silent prayer, I was granted peace of mind. It's as if I'm back in the spirit. That's my blessing. I wouldn't trade peace of mind for the lottery. I'm happy now. God was there all the time. I am calm. That's the best.

For so long, I felt as if I had to be a saint, toting my Bible and wearing my white robe, carrying everyone else. But now I know I don't have to do that. I can just be myself. No more painting on a fake mask for the world.

I've chosen to stay home for now. What I heard when I listened to myself was that I wasn't as strong as I pretended. I needed time to be still, to relax, to pray. I needed a life without work pressure—at least for now. I needed quiet. This was the message I received when I listened to myself. It was a novel experience to hear myself talking. I felt at peace. I was being heard.

Reba: I need applause

After pegging myself as a person who carries, I wondered if I should quit. But after listening to myself, I got a mixed answer. In some cases, the answer was yes. I should quit carrying my adult children and let them fly. But at another level, my searching and listening led me to say, "It's all right to carry some people in my life." I have a need for applause. I need my friends and family to say, "You are fabulous, Reba. How did you think of that? I couldn't have done this without you." The applause is important.

I have a really close lifelong friend named Betty. We grew up together. We have known each other since we were four years old. It's a relationship in which I tend to take care of everything and weigh in on all the decisions. Every problem that besets her is not her problem. It's *our* problem. I set that up when we were just seven years old. When we got our shoes wet at the creek, I figured out how to dry them by placing them in the oven on low before her mother got home. I was always the problem solver. But I enjoy her applause and appreciation, and I always get it from her.

Occasionally, her life gets extremely hectic just when mine seems out of control, too. Maybe I just don't have time to write a letter to her lawyer. When this happens, I might tell her that I can't do it now. Betty might be briefly hurt. But it doesn't last long. She realizes I can't always be there for her. But I don't get any applause either. I miss that.

Listen to Others

Communication doesn't really start until we hear. Active listening is the secret to hearing, being fully alert to the other person. Being there, now. When we listen, others feel valued and significant. That's the gift we give with active listening.

Remove Barriers to Listening

We can't give the gift of active listening if we aren't aware of the barriers that would block our hearing. Some of the most common may sound familiar.

Sarah: Jumping to conclusions

I was a mind reader. I didn't pay much attention to what people said. I was talking when I should have been listening. Even at times when I thought I was listening, I wasn't hearing. When Marvin, in his own disjointed way, was trying to talk to me, I might be watching television or reading.

"You can't be hearing me when you are reading," Marvin would say.

I had heard it all before, so I jumped to the conclusion that I knew what he was going to say before he said it. I never believed it would be any different than the last time. But I now realize that if I had wanted the relationship to work, we had to do something. Perhaps if I had given him my full attention and not jumped to conclusions, the ending would have been different.

Marta: Comparing, not listening

It was hard to listen, because I was always trying to compare: Who is smarter? More competent? More emotionally healthy? Me, or the person speaking? While someone was talking I might be thinking, "Could I do it that well? . . . Do I earn that much? . . . My kids are so much brighter." I couldn't let much in because I was so busy seeing if I measured up. Now I stop my mental conversation when the comparisons start and really listen. Listening is not about comparing. It is about hearing what the person is trying to tell me.

Tamara: Rehearsing my agenda

When I first went into business for myself, I fretted about presentations to potential clients. Often, I was so busy rehearsing what I was going to say, I didn't hear what they were telling me. My whole attention was focused on the preparation and crafting of my next comment. I know now that I missed getting business because of that trait. I didn't hear what the clients wanted. I was too busy rehearsing what I wanted to tell them.

I listen more closely now, without any preconceived notions of the message I am to deliver. Consequently, I hear better. When I listen, the conversation is natural and my remarks are spontaneous and responsive based on what the other person is saying.

Reba: Filtering what I heard

I listened to some things and not to others. My hearing was very selective. I remember one time when I accused Nathan of never complimenting me.

"We're drifting apart," I said. "You never compliment me anymore."

"That's not true," he said, and gave me three examples of compliments he had given me just that morning. As he recounted them, I remembered.

This is only one instance in which I had stopped listening to him and was hearing only what I told myself. I didn't want to hear the truth, so I filled in the blanks, made up my own story, and made it fit. To do that, I filtered what I heard.

It was too late to improve communication and resolve conflicts with my husband. But when I saw the same communications problems leading to conflict with my employees at work, I saw the opportunity to help; not to rush in and save them, but to enable them to save themselves.

When I took off my filters, I saw how pervasive the communication problems were at the office. So I brought in consultants to give seminars to help us all learn how to resolve conflict constructively. Now I can stay out of the driver's seat and don't feel the need to rescue all the time. I can also hear what is truly going on.

Joan: Judging others instantly

I was a judge of people. If I perceived that they were uneducated, if their English was spoken in a backwoods dialect, then I wrote them off. I didn't pay much attention to what they said. I categorized people quickly. If they didn't "fit" me, I smiled politely, but dismissed anything they said. I didn't really listen.

I judged everyone, really. I met a brash young CEO at a reception whom I immediately wrote off as arrogant and materialistic. Sort of a "top gun" type, I thought. And not for me. I made no real attempt to get to know him that evening. But, as fate would have it, two days later, we ended up sitting next to each other on a three-hour flight. I discovered we had a great deal in common, including being fourth cousins. By the time we finished comparing family notes, we were fast friends. He became a client.

I had to learn that by judging people on outward signals, I was missing some of life's nicest surprises. I have put aside my judge's robe. I hear better.

Kate: Interrupting with advice

I never had to hear but a sentence or two before I began offering an overwhelming amount of information and advice. When somebody told me something, what I was hearing in my mind was "Please solve it for me." I realize now that was not necessarily what they were saying. And even if they were, it might not have been appropriate for me to do so.

I've changed my behavior. Now, I look at them and ask, "Are you asking me for an opinion, or are you giving me information, or are you just getting it off your chest?"

Often people just want you to be there. To listen. If they are asking my opinion, I'll say, "Well, I'll tell you what I know, but I'm not going to implement it for you. And what I'm offering may be wrong. It's up to you to decide what to do, and do it."

I still have to remind myself not to jump in and interrupt with advice. But it gets easier as I realize how important it is first just to listen, just to be there.

Michelle: Avoiding the message

I was never a good listener. My aunt and mom told me I was the child who would walk away and sulk when hurt or angry. I could walk around someone forever and never say a word. I just avoided them.

If my husband hurt me, I would calmly get up and go to my

room, and block it out. If I didn't want to hear it, I didn't. But then my feelings got stacked up, higher and higher. Underneath was all this garbage of past hurts.

I had to learn to stay and listen. If I can't stand to hear something I don't want to hear, I've learned to tell the person that I'm too upset to stay right now, but I'll return. Then I come back later and finish the conversation. I don't leave it undone forever.

Communicate for Meaning

When we begin to communicate with others, we are communicating for meaning. What love means to one person may be different for another. Thus, often, when we let go of responsibilities that rightfully belong to another, we get a negative reaction. The person may think we no longer love them. Communicating for the underlying meaning is an important aspect of listening.

Tamara: Aligning communication styles

After Phil and I decided to make a second try at our marriage, we went to a therapist. The therapist was able to identify a major communication gap between us.

Phil came from a home managed (badly) by an alcoholic mother and an absent father. When his salesman father returned on Friday nights to find his wife boozed, arguments would ensue. Arguments in the family were loud, often abusive.

In my family, nobody raised their voice. I never talked about my emotions. If one of us was angry, that was our problem to work out silently. We dealt with it alone. My mom and dad never fought in front of us kids.

Neither Phil nor I realized what an impact our differing backgrounds had on our communication system. When something was really bothering me, I would quietly say to him, "It really upset me when . . ."

What Phil heard was . . . nothing. No screaming, therefore, no message. So, the anger built inside me. And built inside me some more.

On the other hand, when Phil would get angry, he would yell. He was never physically abusive. But the yelling scared me, and I would retreat. I just went out of my way not to anger him. So communication stopped.

Through counseling, we learned to communicate. Phil learned that when I said something, it was important to listen—really listen. I, in turn, quit holding back. I learned to be more up-front and outspoken about my thoughts and feelings. So now we can really hear each other and learn from each other. And we are reaching solutions to problems as they occur, instead of letting them fester and grow in darkness.

Marta: Silence is not golden

Early in our marriage, I sent Joe cards for no reason at all. I might find a funny card and just send it. I never missed sending something for Valentine's Day. Joe never mentioned the cards. So, what's the point, I finally thought. One year, I just stopped sending them. He never mentioned that, either.

I thought, "I'm glad I don't do this anymore, because he doesn't even notice that I quit."

One evening, though, Joe said, "You don't send me cards anymore."

I was in the resentment stage at that point, and responded, "Well, why should I? You don't acknowledge it when I do. I take time out to buy you a card, write something on it, mail it. I'm hoping you'll at least say 'Thanks.' I don't ask for much. Just a simple thank-you. I never got one, so why should I bother to send you a card?"

I guess I really unloaded on him.

Joe looked really surprised. "I just didn't know how to respond," he said. "I really loved getting them. You made me feel special."

After my anger subsided, we finally talked. I realized he really looked forward to getting a card. And Joe finally realized that silence is not golden, at least not in this case. I needed verbal appreciation.

Sarah: Saying, "I need . . ."

At one point I had a manager who was very supportive of my career. I was way overcommitted on projects, as usual, and had no time to shop for clothes to update my spring wardrobe. In fact, I hadn't been spring shopping in two years. I was feeling dowdy and underdressed at all the lunch meetings I was attending.

It was totally out of character for me to complain at work about my personal feelings, but my boss had become a friend as well as my manager, and I remember telling her that I had no time at lunch to shop. I felt as faded as my silk blouses.

She understood. "Get up right now and take the afternoon to shop," she said. "New clothes will make you feel good about yourself. It will give you energy and strength. You'll bring that back to work."

I did. I took all afternoon. As I walked back into the office at 5 P.M., I felt energized. I had two new suits, a new dress, and new blouses. I even had new pumps and a purse. Cinderella had nothing on me. A simple honest comment to my manager had turned her into my fairy godmother.

Joan: No is an option

Allen and I have had a major breakthrough on communication. At one point, I explained how frustrated I got if he said "Yes," but meant "Probably not." He responded by saying that was his way of avoiding my anger. Together we talked it through.

When he realized that I much preferred hearing "No" to a waffly "Yes," he promised to change. I, in turn, said that I would not get angry over any refusal to do a requested chore. It took a lot of effort on both our parts. Allen was in the habit of saying "Yes" and forgot a few times, but he definitely improved. I was hearing "I can't do that" often.

But I was so grateful for the difference that made. We have become real friends, working together. A recent incident at our home points out the quantum leap in our relationship.

Allen and I were outside on the front porch on one of those glorious early spring days. It was planting time. As we looked at our flower garden, we both spotted the spring weeds pushing up in great profusion through the dirt. I had pulled the garden intruders the year before, keeping the beds weed-free.

"I'm not going to pull weeds this year until after I finish this project April 15," I said to Allen.

"Well, I'm not going to pull them either." Allen said. "I won't have time."

We talked about who else might. We didn't have any great ideas on that, so we just looked at each other, and Allen grinned. "Looks like we might have a lot of weeds in our flowers," he said. I laughed and agreed.

This level of communication is a giant step forward for us. Before, I would have been silently hoping he would do it. He probably would have been silently hoping I would. In the end, we might have been irritated with each other because it didn't get done. Instead, we felt like coconspirators in a plan to create a certain level of mayhem. We were in this together, and it felt great.

Kate: Hey, they *can* understand

One of my earliest recognitions that some of my problems stemmed from not listening happened when I was working as a branch administrator. When the sales director gave me the "Bitch, bitch, bitch" mug for Christmas, I realized that neither carrying nor bitching made any sense for solving problems. I was stressed and miserable, so I started going to counseling.

The therapist helped me shift my perspective. I was finally able to ask myself, "What's best for everybody?"

I began to ask questions at the office and discovered that the salespeople were not trying to be difficult. They really didn't know how to fill out the forms correctly. So I began to work with them and train them, and everyone changed. Their orders got better and better. And my mood was so wonderful that they asked me if I was on drugs! That was a compliment. I had come a long way from the woman with the high standards and deaf ears.

Create Safe Circles

Safe circles are very important to making new choices. We need people with whom we connect, who share our values and moral principles. A safe circle of friends that you can trust is absolutely mandatory.

Safe circles begin with a common interest. I call them connectors. We do not connect with material symbols, like money or résumés. We connect with our shared humanity—love of family, the life challenges we have all faced, moments of crisis, the grief when we lose a loved one. These are what we all have in common.

Connectors are the commonalities of living we share as human beings. I witnessed a wonderful example of connecting at a business meeting between an American businessman and his Japanese counterparts. The American was there to discuss a possible sale of his company's products. Looking around the table, he wondered what they all had in common. Since he knew very little about the other men at the table, he spotted only one common characteristic. They all had at least some gray hair. My friend reached in his jacket and pulled out his wallet, producing pictures of his grandchildren. He began to pass them around. The other men smiled and soon were passing around pictures of their grandchildren. The meeting went well. My friend had found a connection.

From connectors, we move into trust. Trust is earned. As we

prove our integrity, our trustworthiness, we find ourselves earning trust from others. Smart women generally are trusted women because they can be counted on. Our safe circles are built within groups of people we can truly trust. Love may be unconditional, but trust is earned.

Safe circles may be personal, professional, or spiritual.

- *Personal Circles:* Personal circles can be long friendships, family and support systems. The people in this circle do not care what you do for a living. Often people in my personal circle are clueless as to what my job actually entails. My mother is a strong supporter in my personal circle, but ask her what I do and she can't explain my work.

  Someone recently gave me the best example of a personal circle that I've heard. Susan was going through a difficulty in her marriage and was unable to continue living in a normal manner. She was too upset. She called her best friend in despair. Her friend came over, but Susan didn't want to talk. They went for a walk, not talking, but just walking together. That silent support got Susan over the emotional trauma of the moment and gave her the strength she needed right then.

  With a personal circle, you are one with someone and can just *be*. No justification needed.

- *Professional Circles:* Professional circles are generally created around our job or business interests. This circle becomes invaluable in today's changing business environment. Connecting to individuals within and without our workplace is critical.

  Roberta was an executive for a major corporation. When her company first began restructuring, Roberta called the trusted people who made up her professional circle. They gave her advice, encouragement, and job leads. When she was downsized, her pro-

fessional circle helped her find a job within three weeks. She is
now a senior manager for a midsize company.

- *Spiritual Circles:* Spiritual circles are shared by people with similar
  beliefs. They may be of the same religion, or they may not. The
  critical component is that everyone in this circle shares the same
  values. This circle can become extremely close as lives change.
  Members of the circle feel free to share their lives and grow.

  I participate in a Bible study group. We became a spiritual
  circle. We are from different backgrounds, different religions, different geographic locations, and different professions. Most people
  in this group have little knowledge of what I do professionally.
  But this group consistently offers unconditional support and
  guidance. They have become an anchor for me and for others in
  the group. We are spiritually connected.

  We may tend to see these circles as separate compartments
  of life. But our lives overlap in all areas. When our circles overlap,
  they gather strength and synergy.

  Although families might seem a natural safe circle, that is
  not always the case. Michelle found that out the hard way. Sometimes when change is needed, families are the last to notice and
  support it.

Michelle: Siblings too close

When I tried to commit suicide by not going to dialysis, it was a wake-
up call for my family. My brother and sister were devastated. I had been
trying to tell them I was on the edge, but they weren't listening. They
kept telling me how "strong" I was. To them, that was me—strong
Michelle.

They couldn't imagine I needed help. Ironically, my family
couldn't help me because they were too close. They just couldn't believe I

was so down. They would tell me just to be the same strong person I always was. And they would smother me with love, but it wasn't a listening love. It was a "Michelle-as-usual" love. They couldn't see me any other way.

Find People to Trust

Michelle is not alone. Many of us have to create safe circles. We have to find people we trust. We need safe circles for support and encouragement in the good times and tough ones. We need honest feedback as we contemplate new choices. We need input in times of decision. And we need a safe circle to celebrate with us when we make progress on our new choices. Each woman felt that creating safe circles was a necessary step for her change.

Michelle: Finding family connections

Finding people who genuinely accept you the way you are is not easy. When most of my family, and even the doctors, did not understand that I was going under, I found an aunt and an uncle who did. My uncle is a minister and a missionary. He could see the danger signs. When I got desperate, I picked up the phone, called them, and started to cry. They were right with me. They prayed with me. They propped up my sagging spiritual foundation. I called them many times over the next two months. They were always right there.

Tamara: Starting women's and couples' circles

The first safe circle I deliberately set out to create was a women's group. The group is about three years old now. It's an open group, and some women have come and gone. But for six of us, it really works. We meet twice a month in each other's homes and take turns facilitating the meeting. The group isn't just for socializing. We are there to grow. We listen to each other. Confidentiality is a rule. We've gotten really close. We are relaxed and informal. I know we've helped each other through some major challenges.

Phil and I then started a couples' group with several husbands and wives from our church. We meet every other Sunday night. Once again, we are there to share and support, not to socialize. I know this group means a lot to Phil. He feels a part of the church now in a way he didn't before. I don't think men often have groups in which they can share who they are and what they want. It's been a blessing for all of us.

Now, I am attempting to form a new group. One of the women in our couples' group is an artist. I've read where artists do their best work in colonies, rather than alone. I want to pursue my fine art and painting again. I am hoping we can form the nucleus of an artist's safe circle in our small town.

I know from experience that when I start out to form a new safe circle, some will come for a season and fall away. That is all right. Those who stay will begin to develop the deep trust that creates bonds that last forever.

Marta: Creating circles at work

Without my support groups, I could never put events into perspective. I formed a safe circle at work composed of several other Hispanic women. We use each other as a sounding board. If I am feeling a certain way about a work issue, I can bounce it off them. Am I the only one feeling this way? Do my concerns have validity?

We coach each other. One woman right now wants more exposure to senior-level management. I have that exposure, so I'm her coach on how to do that from her position. I give her ideas on what she might do to accomplish that goal. Other times, I ask her for her perspective on something I am working on. I find her opinion very valuable.

I don't look at these women as mentors. I see them as peers, regardless of our individual titles. We have similar interests, thoughts, the same values. We can be completely honest without thinking of repercussions. It's a real safety net for me.

Accept Honest Feedback
Safe circles allow us to hear honest feedback we ask for and feedback we don't. We have given permission for others to be candid with us.

Sarah: Encouragement for change

I am so independent. It's been hard to let people in. I was always concerned about my professional appearance. It was important to me to appear to be in control. I didn't want to appear weak. It's been hard for me to trust.

I do have a safe circle composed of three girlfriends. I think they found me first. They were really honest with me from the start. So I can be really honest with them. One of them invited the group to go on a four-day cruise together. I was still married at the time. I had never taken a vacation without Marvin. It was a daring idea. But after much thought, I went.

The cruise was the start of a soul-searching journey for the four of us. I spent most of the time sleeping in my cabin. I was physically exhausted from work, and mentally exhausted from not knowing how to handle the unresolved issues in my life. My circumstances were not that different from those of the others. All of us were the financial and emotional bedrock of our families. We were handling tremendous responsibilities, and in that process, unfortunately, we had all outgrown our marriages. None of us knew what to do next.

When I finally emerged from my cabin the last night, all of us sat at dinner and concluded we had to do something positive to change our lives. And on the spot, we formed a safe circle. We gave each other permission to bare our souls. Then, we helped each other figure out what each of us individually could commit to immediately to make our miserable selves get moving.

I committed publicly to a healthier me. I wasn't ready to deal with my marriage, although I knew we had problems. I could, however, deal with my fat body. And with the encouragement of my newfound support group, I did just that. After I got home, I found a time to exercise each day. I switched to low-fat snacks and learned how to eat wisely on a traveler's schedule. And I made progress. My weight went down and my energy went up.

We grew closer. My safe circle encouraged me when I decided finally to leave my marriage behind. Without them, I don't know that I would ever have done that. For three years they were asking, "Why do you take the verbal abuse? Why do you take the infidelity?" I didn't have a good answer. It made me think.

They saw me through. After my divorce, Marvin was constantly calling, and whining about not having any money. He asked for loans. At first, the old me wanted to help out. I somehow felt it was my fault. My safe circle began to send me postcards saying, "Don't do it." I was getting one card a day from them for a while.

Their support kept me from caving in to my old behavior to fix it and make it all right for Marvin. I was glad when I got a call from the bank asking for payment on an overdue note. I discovered Marvin had forged my signature on a loan. Thank you, ladies, I thought. I can't bail this man out. He's got to learn on his own.

Reba: Truth without personal gain

I have several really, really good friends. What I call a really, really good friend is one who tells you the truth, not cruelly, but the truth nonetheless, when you ask. And they tell you the truth without personal gain. That's rare.

I have lots of friends, but it's so easy for all of us to respond based on our self-interest. Let me explain. I'm divorced. Suppose I were to tell my single girlfriends that I was thinking of getting engaged, or, heaven forbid, married? Well, they begin to think, "Oh no, there goes our social group. There goes Saturday at Reba's condo." There is that little human element that creeps into our advice, centered around what's best for me, as well as the person asking for feedback.

But that doesn't stop me. I'm a gatherer of information. I always listen, but I don't always agree. I just gather up the different perspectives and make my own decisions.

My mother is my best source. Her advice is absolutely unbiased in her own favor. She sticks with what is best for me. She's very valuable to me. She knows me so well that sometimes she'll tell me what's best knowing full well I won't do it.

"Well, Reba. You ought to put that poor old dog out of his misery. But, ha! Fat chance that will happen."

Once we have let loose, opened our minds and our ears, it's a natural occurrence to find our hearts opening as well. It takes us back where we started—our desire to love and be loved.

Choose to Listen

These women choose to listen in new ways that you can also use:

- Quiet your inner dialogue
- Listen to who you are
- Overcome blocks to listening
- Listen to others without judgment
- Ask questions to clarify meaning
- Communicate feelings and expectations

- Recognize the needs of others
- Accept disagreement
- Live in the present moment
- Seek others for sharing and support

Your Story

What are some ways you can better listen to yourself?

What can you do to improve how you listen to others?

How can you create or expand your safe circles?

Chapter 9
Choose to Love

Is there anyone who wouldn't choose to love? Of course not. But somewhere on the road to carrying we lost our sense of what love is about. We misused love and it became a burden. We thought we were loving, but we were controlling. We thought we were giving, but we were taking.

We need to start over.

Loving starts with ourselves. If we don't love ourselves, we cannot love another. Choosing to love means choosing to love ourselves with the same generosity of spirit that makes love from another so special.

Love is not conditional. Love is not controlling. Love is not obligatory. Love flows out of our deep sense of self, of knowing and loving ourselves. Some of us were raised in families where love was conditional, and maybe we haven't developed a clear sense of loving. We think it comes with strings attached. It doesn't.

We are capable of learning new ways to love. It starts with self.

Jesus said the second great commandment was to "love thy neighbor as thyself." Does this not imply that we must love ourselves purely, unselfishly, unconditionally? Otherwise, what kind of love would we be offering our neighbor? We don't love ourselves only when we fulfill our expectations, e.g., when we lose ten pounds. That kind of love comes with strings attached. If we fail, does that mean we won't love ourselves? Often, that is just how we treat ourselves. We berate ourselves when we fall short of our own expectations.

So, choosing to love means choosing to nurture ourselves, to love ourselves without judgment, to encourage ourselves when events seem dismal, to make time for self-care, to find humor in our difficulties, to celebrate joy in the moment, and to give to others but also to receive from those others help in kind. This is love, and it starts with you.

1. Love ourselves

Learning to love ourselves means learning to forgive our past mistakes, listening inside, recognizing our needs and acknowledging them, and understanding the unique gifts we bring to the world.

2. Love others

Loving others is a natural outgrowth of loving ourselves. As we love ourselves, we understand the uniqueness of each individual and what they offer to us and the world. As we have compassion for ourselves, we find we have compassion for others.

Loving others is a principle of life in every major religion. The following list shows this to be true.

- All things whatsoever ye would that men should do to you, do so even so to them, for this is the law and the prophets. (**Christianity**—King James Bible)
- Injure not others, in the manner that they would injure you. (**Buddhism**—*Udana-Varga*)
- Here certainly is the golden maxim: do not do to others that

which we do not want them to do to us. (**Confucianism**—
Analects)

- That which you hold as detestable, do not do to your neighbor.
  That is the whole Law: the rest is but commentary. (**Judaism**—
  Talmud)
- None of you is a believer if he does not desire for his brother that
  which he desires for himself. (**Islam**—*Sunna*)
- That nature alone is good which checks itself from doing to others
  that which would not be good for itself. (**Zoroastrianism**—
  Dadistan-i-kinik)
- Consider that your neighbor gains your gain and that your neigh-
  bor loses that which you lose. (**Taoism**—*T'ai Shang Kan Ying
  Pien*)
- Such is the sum of duty: do not do to others that which, to you,
  would do harm to yourself. (**Hinduism**—*Mahabharata*)

3. Love life

Loving life means trusting your inner voice, following your path,
and rejoicing every day in the good that comes to you. Gratitude is an important part of loving life. So is a sense of adventure.

Love Ourselves

Loving ourselves does not come easily, at least for me. I always felt a great
deal of pressure to keep my business growing. So I put in long hours and
added continually to my work load. I guess I shouldn't have been surprised when, after my annual checkup, my doctor prescribed one thing: a
two-week vacation.

"Take two weeks, Hattie," he said. "Not your usual one-week or
five-day vacation. You have the body of a twenty-eight-year-old, but the
mind of a sixty-eight-year-old. You are weary. It's like a slow bleed. If you

don't stop it now, your emotional exhaustion will impact you physically."

I needed to learn to love myself, the Hattie inside that loves to be with people, to hug and laugh and goof off with friends. So I made one major decision. I closed my office for the last two weeks in December.

I am in the speaking business. The last two weeks of December is a slow time for my business anyway. We might get a few phone calls from people asking for information on our seminar and training programs, but little else. There is no compelling reason we have to stay open.

And I love Christmas! It is my favorite holiday. I love decorating my home. I love going home to be with family. I love shopping for my friends and family. Giving myself permission to take two weeks really to enjoy Christmas was loving myself. I still have a ways to go to treat myself with the loving kindness I deserve during the other fifty weeks, but I'm grateful for progress.

So are others.

Tamara: Release joy

When Phil and I were first married, I went through a period of deep depression. To this day, I don't really know why. I know I felt inadequate compared to Phil. Phil is quite outgoing and charismatic. By the time we had been married a few months, he had been invited to sit on several community boards and was getting lots of business. I was still working at the insurance agency and going to school. I didn't feel particularly accomplished in spite of my grueling schedule. And I am quiet by nature, not outgoing.

What pulled me out of the depression was keeping a journal. I am not a writer, and I haven't written much since that time. But every day, on the bus into town, I wrote in my journal. I put down my darkest, deepest emotions and feelings. Anger surfaced. Already, early in the marriage, I felt I was pulling more than my weight. My feelings of inadequacy surfaced; so too did my resentment at Phil's mother's irrational outbursts. And some feelings from childhood that I had never dealt with surfaced. It was a pretty bleak journal.

But as I continued to write, my depression lightened. It was as if by getting it out in the open, at least out of the deep recesses of my mind and onto paper, I was exposing all those negative thoughts to the light. And the light, amazingly, erased them.

I can remember sitting on the bus one day, and realizing, with a clarity that left no room for doubt, that love is the answer, the antidote to the world's ills. I suddenly felt compassion for my husband, rather than envy. I found loving others, including my mother-in-law, a natural response, not a forced one. But most of all, I loved myself. There was such joy that accompanied loving myself. I discovered you can't really love another until you love yourself.

I rediscovered my church during this time. Now, I start each day with centering meditation and prayer. Letting go of my thoughts and resting in a place of inner quiet has made a significant difference in my life. I find it is possible to get beyond my gnawing everyday concerns and experience instead a sense of calmness, clarity, and deep well-being. If I miss that quiet time, I feel it.

I am an artist, and I discovered I also needed to make time for my creative self. One day, I had an artist friend come over and give me an oil-painting lesson, right in the middle of a workweek. I put all my clients aside and just did it. It felt great!

It's little things, like taking a walk in the middle of the day, that help. One Saturday, I went for a long hike through the woods. I love to be outdoors. It puts me back in touch with who I am. I felt so loved doing that for myself. It's not just cherishing others that's important. It's cherishing myself, too.

Loving myself has given me permission to nurture myself. What a difference it makes! The other night I was so tired. I was planning to work, but I just did not want to work any longer. So, I gave myself permission to quit. I turned off the computer and put on some gospel music. And I began to do a meditative walk around the living room. I went in a circle and just walked slowly, one foot down, then picking up the other foot, in a slow, rhythmic pattern. It sounds silly, but I enjoyed it. I walked, totally immersed in the music, and then went to bed. I woke up completely refreshed and filled with creative ideas for my work.

Sarah: Flowers from me

Learning to love myself is an important breakthrough. I have never allowed myself to take any time for me. One of the books I took time out to read celebrated womanhood each day. Well, after reading one day I decided I had not acknowledged myself in a very long time. I sent myself flowers. I love flowers, and I seldom receive them.

I ordered simple flowers wrapped in plain paper. I asked for daffodils, but the florist convinced me that was not a simple request in January, so I settled for carnations. When others in the office asked who sent the flowers, I found myself replying, "Someone who tends to take me for granted." I had the nicest, warmest, secret glow inside, even warmer than if a friend had sent them. I do tend to take myself for granted, and it felt really nice to appreciate myself. It made me feel more loving toward everyone.

Kate: Calm mind, calm body

I received one of my greatest compliments recently from a new client. In the midst of a very stressful time for her, she commented, "No matter what's happening, you're always so calm."

Calm? Me? Yes, she was right. I had come a very long way from the frantic woman I was before who never took time to care for herself. She wanted to know how I got there. Not overnight, I explained. One thought at a time.

My life had been in chronic overdrive. My mind raced and my muscles were always tense. It wasn't until my car wreck and back injury that I was forced to slow down and learn how to relax. The first thing I tried was biofeedback. When the therapist attached me to the equipment, the recorded muscle tension was so high she thought the equipment was broken. Three machines later, she realized it was me. My muscles were like rocks. It took months of practice even to know what a relaxed muscle felt like, but, boy, did it feel good.

My body had finally learned how to be still, but my mind was still on overdrive. So I practiced other approaches such as meditation, focusing, hypnosis, and prayer. With time and practice, I learned to take time daily to quiet my thoughts and make a space for hearing me. When worrisome thoughts came to mind, I countered them with positive thoughts of gratitude, hope, and humor. With time, the negative attitudes rarely came.

I'm finally taking care of myself. I do feel calm. I am thankful for the compliment.

Joan: Forgive myself

Do we, as mothers, ever forgive ourselves for the mistakes we've made in raising our children? It's so easy to look back from the vantage point of maturity and see how you might have done things differently. I had to learn that holding on to past regrets was interfering with loving myself. I have a grown son. He's a good citizen, not a drug addict or criminal, but in many ways he seems unprepared for life. At twenty-two, he has returned home to live while he finishes school and tries to start a new career. In many ways, he seems to live in a world of fantasy, always thinking that he will get the "big break." He is emotionally fragile.

It's easy to blame ourselves for our children's problems. I can think of plenty of events I would have handled differently. I was frightened of my husband's temper and intimidated by his need for control. To keep peace, I lived his life down to the last detail, but I lost my sense of self in that process. I was depressed. I could barely meet my own needs, much less those of my small children. I could barely get out of bed in the mornings because of that depression. I can now think of times when I should have been a better nurturer for a small child.

But I have learned something else recently. I have learned not only to love that small child that needed to be held more. I have learned to love that frightened young woman who thought the only way to survive was to give in completely to her husband's demands. She needed nurturing, too, and was without. She did her best at the level of maturity she had then. She loved her children. She never hurt them, and she fed them, read to them, and cuddled them when she could. She meant well. And I forgave her for not knowing enough to stand up for herself sooner, for not challenging the control of one person over another. I forgave her for not being a perfect mother. She simply didn't know how, but she wanted to be. And in forgiving that young woman, I had compassion for that young, frightened woman, and I loved myself.

From that vantage point, I can love my son better today. He, too, is operating from his level of understanding and means well. He, too, will grow in maturity and life skills. He, too, will need to be able to forgive the young man and cherish the new man as he grows.

Forgiving myself is a most important ingredient in loving myself. Now, I can forgive others, too. I have forgiven the misguided young husband who thought if he could just control everything, life would be good. He, too, is a wiser and gentler man today. Life teaches us well, if we but listen and learn and love.

Marta: Love my body

I knew I should exercise. I just had a million reasons why I couldn't do it that day. Too much to do, usually. Or it was raining. Or cold. Or I forgot my gym bag. Any excuse would do. But as I have been actively concentrating on making time for me, that is changing. In learning to love my-self, I *want* to exercise. That's a major shift in my thinking—from *should* exercise to *want to* exercise. I find that when I exercise, it's just a wonder-ful feeling. I find as I return to work after exercising, I often have a whole new perspective on my work.

One day I spent forty minutes on the treadmill during lunch. Normally, I might drudge through fifteen minutes, but that day I just got into the rhythm and didn't want to quit. When I stopped, I realized how long it had been. I was shocked! I had no idea I could walk that long without straining. I didn't feel any guilt about how long I had been on the treadmill. I just felt really good.

When I got home, I was still excited. I told my husband, "Guess what I did? I did forty minutes on the treadmill and I could have kept going."

Joe could feel my excitement. He said, "There's something going on with you, and it makes me feel closer to you."

The love I'm developing for me spills over naturally to everyone else. I'm learning that if I don't take care of myself, there's no way to take care of the people around me. Not that I don't still struggle with guilt. I still ask, If I allow myself to do this, what is the consequence? Am I let-ting things drop? What is the perception of others? But as I go ahead, I find very little drops, and I feel so good that I am effective in new ways.

Reba: A great beginning

I was so lucky to have my mom. She believed I could do anything, and she clearly conveyed that message to me. She also gave me free rein to prove that true. I grew up loving myself, who I was, what I could do. The world appeared to me to be a place of unlimited possibilities.

In college, the only full scholarship I was offered was to a second-rate state teachers college. The college didn't even offer the subject

I wanted for my major. But a full scholarship was not to be ignored, so I went.

The courses were easy. I soon found that by reading the textbooks, I could score 100 on the tests. I quit attending classes, and spent my free time picking out my own reading material from the library. At semester's end, I was surprised to find I made all B's, instead of A's. I had been graded down for nonattendance.

Infuriated, I packed my bags, withdrew from the college, and returned home. My mom didn't blink an eye. "You deserve better" was her only comment. "You'll find the money to go somewhere else. You can do anything."

And I did. Loving myself came easily because of the great freedom and unwavering love I got as a child.

Love Others

When we love ourselves, it is a short step to loving others, a natural progression. I had an assistant who loved bells. Linda was a special person who went out of her way to help me. I loved her. On every trip, I would bring back a souvenir bell for her from that location. Once, on an international flight, I was lined up to get on the plane when I realized I had forgotten to get Linda a bell. I jumped out of line and ran back to the airport gift shop. I bought a bell and ran back to my flight. It was worth it, because I so appreciated her. I really would have felt bad if I hadn't had that bell for her.

It's little wonder I loved Linda. She would climb a mountain if needed to make sure our work went smoothly. I remember one incident in particular. I was scheduled to give a seminar in Jamaica. I was having breakfast with the seminar organizers on a Sunday morning after my arrival on that Caribbean island.

"Good news!" my breakfast companion said. The "good news"

was that twice as many participants were attending the seminar as the sponsors had expected. But while I was nodding my head and smiling, my stomach was in knots. The seminar started in two days, and I suddenly needed twice as many workbooks as I had prepared and brought with me. I saw disaster looming in spite of all my best intentions to make sure everything went smoothly.

After breakfast, I raced back to my hotel room and called Linda, who was at home getting ready for church on a Sunday morning.

"No problem," Linda said. "I'll just change my clothes, head to the office, put together one hundred and fifty more packages and send them by overnight mail to you."

That was not an easy task. Each package was one hundred pages long and involved getting a rush order to the local print shop, then assembling the workbooks complete with an array of promotional giveaways. Linda got it to the overnight delivery service on a special order at 2 A.M. That was an act of love.

Give unto Others

Giving to others means helping another in a moment of need, supporting someone's efforts to move forward, sharing what we know, and viewing the world from another's perspective. But giving does not mean carrying. In respecting the individuality of each person, and trusting that person to find his or her own path, we can love unconditionally without taking on the responsibility of another.

Marta: A new understanding

Man, I used to sizzle inside when I saw Joe pop a movie in about the time I arrived home from work. I felt the same way about his habit of eating a leisurely breakfast and reading the paper as if the rest of us weren't going nuts trying to get out of the house and to the office.

"What right does he have to do that?" I wondered. At one level, I understood that he did work long hours, and generally worked weekends. On the other hand, I didn't exactly consider my weekend schedule of shopping, cleaning, and carpooling a retreat.

After I began to take some time for myself, though, I gained a new view of Joe's movie escapes. After I began to use my lunch hours as a retreat to love myself, I had an entirely new perspective. The time I took to exercise and write in my journal changed my life. My newfound creativity and my renewed energy fed me and made every portion of my life more enjoyable, even the chores. I now understand how important it was for Joe to have time for himself, too.

Instead of resenting the time Joe spent watching a movie or reading the paper, I understood that his personal time kept him at his best. A major source of resentment was removed with no change in his behavior, just a change in my perspective.

Sarah: Boosting morale

At work, we always have an off-site session to do our yearly business planning. This particular year, morale was really low. Many changes were coming, and you could just feel everyone asking, "Will I be here in six months? If so, will I still *want* to be here?"

I sensed what was going on. It would be hard to plan anything in that atmosphere of uncertainty. Then I had an idea. I found a store that specialized in motivational posters and unusual cards and such. I bought little cards that were unique to each person and that highlighted something positive about their contribution to the department. The gifts were a huge hit. It really made the point that each of us brought something valuable and creative to the group. And it turned the atmosphere around. Everyone just pitched in and planned as if we knew exactly what would happen that year. The meeting was very productive.

I actually didn't know that would be the result. I just wanted everyone to feel loved and wanted, regardless of what that year might hold for any of us. I felt encouraged, too.

Michelle: Sharing my story

My long desire to do volunteer work came in an unexpected way. I was the "grandmother" of dialysis with twenty years of living through treatment. I knew more about dialysis than even the staff at the treatment centers. Certainly, I had experienced every side effect, every challenge failed kidneys can inflict. My story became a role model for others—and my gift to them.

The other patients at dialysis began coming to me often. They just wanted to talk and to ask questions. So I started a patient group at the treatment center. I listened to the group's fears. I told them my experience. One day, a man whose name I didn't even know came up to me and hugged me and said, "You are the most special woman I know."

That hug was a healing of the soul for me, too.

Sarah: Be with you, be with me

My problem has been that I am willing to give but not so willing to receive. I never expected anything from anybody. It's really an act of self-will. I always said, "I will do it myself."

Since I left home at age eighteen, I have never asked my mother for anything. Not even for sympathy. She would call and I would say that everything was fine, even if it wasn't. But she knew. She really knew when I was having a hard time with Marvin. But she couldn't help because I didn't share with her. I have finally realized that part of the gift you give people is letting them into your life. Letting them know what you need.

At one point, my mother had surgery. I didn't even know until afterwards. I was very upset that not one member of my family had told me she was in the hospital. I guess it made me feel insignificant. She may not have needed me, but I wanted to be needed. I felt cheated because I wasn't there to help.

So a few months later, when I had surgery, I had learned my lesson. I let her know in advance that I was going to have my knee repaired. She came to be with me. I didn't really have to have her help, but she wanted to be there. I'm finally realizing that loving others includes letting them in and not always saying, "I can do this myself."

Joan: A pinch of nutmeg, a dash of love

My mother-in-law broke her hip and can't do all she used to do. At Thanksgiving, she would traditionally cook for us. Cooking was very important to her. She was an excellent cook, and she could count on our rave reviews of her Thanksgiving feast. This year, however, my sisters-in-law and I told her we would cook. She was not happy. We could tell she felt useless. Not being able to cook was hard for her to accept.

We came up with an idea that worked great. We took a chair and placed it in the center of the kitchen. Then we sat Mama on it, and she directed.

"Add a little more salt."

"Now put in a pinch of nutmeg."

She liked the director's role. Being part of the action was very important for her. It made a fun afternoon. Rather than feeling bad about Mama being on the couch watching television, we had a glorious time, laughing and joking with her. The kitchen sang with love.

Reba: The purse

I learned an important lesson about giving early on when I was carrying my friend Jenny in college. We were so poor, and Jenny was even poorer than I, since she was often unemployed. Well, on one occasion I decided she had to have some money. I decided this in my head. She didn't ask me for money. But I thought she was desperate. So, I gave her ten dollars. Ten dollars was a lot of money to me, and to Jenny, too. We were feeding ourselves and our two children on five dollars a week.

I'm not sure what I thought she was going to do with it. But I couldn't have been more surprised than when she walked in my apartment to show me her purchase. A purse! I thought the woman was starving and when I gave her ten dollars, she bought a purse. She was thrilled with her purchase. It was a fifty-dollar purse she had bought on sale for ten—a very expensive purse for 1968. I was astounded.

Later, that incident served as an important lesson for me. The money had been a gift. I hadn't told Jenny what to do with it. It was a gift without strings. The fact that I had been outraged at how she decided to spend that gift was taking away from the unconditional nature of the offering. I realized I really wanted the gift to be unconditional. I still feel that way. Any gift I give is unconditional, no strings attached. I still remember how pleased she was at her great buy, and my surprise at how she used that ten dollars. The gift, to me, has been the chuckle I've had at myself all these years. Now, I no longer make assumptions about how a gift will be used. It's made giving a much richer experience.

Marta: No tax receipts

A couple of years ago, we were having a really cold winter for our part of the country. As I was driving to work, the radio was talking about the homeless being cold, and needing coats. I thought about those people standing out in the weather, and I just couldn't shake the image I got. So, when I got to work, I told my friends and coworkers, "I'm willing to collect coats, scarves, hats, and mittens, and take them to the shelter, if you will give something. No junk." I thought that would be demeaning. I also said that I wasn't going to give out any tax receipts. That wasn't the purpose for this trip.

I went through my closets and found I had coats I was keeping for sentimental reasons. I didn't really wear them. We collected forty-five coats, and I don't know how many hats, mittens, and scarves. As I drove up to the homeless shelter, I was filled head to toe with my own special sort of warmth. That warmth was *my* gift, and I can still feel it today.

Kate: The Can Man

I had stopped at a convenience store to get some milk late on the Friday before Christmas. It was dark. As I got in my car, a young man got out of his dented pickup truck and started picking up empty aluminum cans in the parking lot. As he picked up each one, he almost lovingly wiped it off and put it in his sack. As I watched, I noticed he limped. His clothes were old and his hair was combed but not clean. Soon the man crossed the street and started picking up cans on the median. I felt I was being "called" to reach out to him.

I generally have a lot of empty soft drink cans in the car, but I was disappointed to find only three this time. But three might help, so I drove my car to where he was.

When I offered the cans, he was tearful and put his hand to his chest. With some difficulty he stuttered, "Th . . . Th . . . Thank . . . y . . . y . . . you. . . . What a nice thing to do for me."

I was touched. Remembering I had a barrel of cans at home waiting to be recycled, I offered to meet him in a grocery-store parking lot near my home with the cans. After some confusion about where to go, he agreed.

There weren't as many as I expected at home, but I quickly gathered them up and returned to the parking lot where I found him waiting. I gave him the small bag of cans and ten dollars in an envelope.

He said, "Wa . . . wa . . . wait. Wh . . . wh . . . what . . . is this? I can't take money from you. You might need it."

I assured him that God had blessed me with a good income this year and that my gift to him was an expression of my gratitude to God and of God's love for him.

He looked at me intently for a moment. Then he started to tell me his story. "Why did you do this for me . . . ? When I see the ladies in a store . . . they look away . . . and leave quickly. I see the ladies . . . with their pretty babies . . . and wish I had a wife and babies," he said. He was tearing. "Thank you for being nice."

He told me that he lived with his brother, who owned the truck he was in, and picked up cans to supplement his disability check. He thanked me over and over for my gift. Then he said, "I also like . . . hugs," and smiled.

I hugged him and he hugged me back tightly. His hug for me was much greater than the gift I had given him. I reached out to give love to a stranger and he touched my life.

When I shared the story of the Can Man with my friends, they were terrified that I might have been killed. After all, I had no idea who this man was, and he stuttered and was dirty.

But I had listened to the small voice inside and felt totally safe to reach out. I knew that this was what loving my neighbor was really all about.

Relearn to Play

Play is an important component of sharing love and of joy. To play is to laugh, to release our natural spontaneity, to create joy in the moment.

Tamara: Unrehearsed dancing

One Saturday morning, our seven-year-old son had a friend over. I was working, but suddenly had a strong desire to be with the children. I decided it was an angel message, so I listened.

I went into the room where they were watching cartoons. I turned on some loud music and began to dance. They joined me, and we just danced as hard as we could, free movement, fast and furious, until we were on the floor laughing and exhausted. We lay on the floor and I began taking them through a visualization exercise of floating up and going out into space and going to heaven. We visualized people who had died and then we saw God. He took us up on His lap and put His arms around us and told us He loved us. The scenario just came. None of it was planned. Once I let go and just started getting into it, it swelled up and just grew of its own accord. The boys loved it. Then we got out the drums and were drumming to some music. We had the best time together.

It's like my little kid came out to play. It can be very hard to get her out to play. She doesn't always want to do that. So, that was a special morning I'll always remember. I suspect the two boys will, too.

Reba: I don't do night movies

I was dating someone new. I really hadn't been dating in a long time. One evening he asked me to go to the movies. I said, "I don't do night movies."

He looked at me as if I was crazy. "Why?" he asked. "Do you think it's dangerous?"

"No," I replied. "I just always go in the afternoons."

My response was automatic. I go to movies in the afternoon, usually with girlfriends. I had been doing that for so long I just automatically said I don't go to movies at night, as if it were a tenet for living akin to "I don't do drugs."

Later I realized how ridiculous that must have sounded to him. I was stuck in an old routine that had no real foundation for becoming a rule in my life.

The next time we were together I suggested a night movie. I had a great time. I felt like it was a real adventure.

Marta: Two days in the dirt

Joe is very spontaneous. I remember coming home on a Friday evening to find my husband in the driveway with the truck packed, the tent trailer hooked up to the back, and everyone ready to leave for a camping trip.

"Hi, honey," he said. "The children and I thought a camp-out would be fun. The weather's great. Throw your stuff together and we'll leave in five minutes."

Well, my response was less than enthusiastic. But what choice did I have? Here stood our children looking at me expectantly. They had obviously spent two hours getting the camping gear out and packed. They had been to the grocery store. The children were dancing around excitedly.

I growled under my breath to Joe, "Couldn't you give me a little more advance notice, so I could prepare mentally for spending two days in the dirt?" And we left, with me silently cursing Joe, the universe, and my fate in life.

But I've gotten better. As I've learned to love myself, I've also grown to love Joe's spontaneity, his joy in the moment, and his receptivity to that joy. My appreciation of him has really grown.

This spring I returned home to find the truck packed again. But Joe had done me a favor this time. He had called before I left work and when I answered the phone I heard a tape of "Green Acres." I laughed. I knew what that meant. And I knew that his warning me was an act of love on his part. Our two days in the dirt were filled with joy. We stargazed, hiked, saw deer and a coyote, counted birds, and arrived home refreshed and rejuvenated.

Rediscover Dating and Romance

For couples, dating and romance is a form of play often neglected in busy lives.

Joan: Leave guilt behind

Allen and I took a trip alone together for the first time since our honeymoon thirteen years earlier. We had always taken the children with us. Only the youngest was still at home, but still that ugly guilt raised its head and said, "You can't do this. How can you go to this part of the country and not let her enjoy it also?"

This was the first time in years we even had an opportunity to travel alone. A friend volunteered to keep Angela.

Anyway, we both experienced these guilty feelings at the beginning of our trip. "Oh, isn't this wonderful! Too bad Angela's not here to see this."

But as the week progressed, we discovered each other again. We began just to enjoy each other's company in a way we hadn't done in so long, we had forgotten we could. The evenings were very romantic. We watched the sun set over the Pacific. We took long walks. We enjoyed quiet nights alone talking and kissing and enjoying the intimacy of being alone.

We swore when we returned that we'd take another vacation together—alone, and soon.

Finding another opportunity for a vacation alone hasn't happened yet. But we do find time to play together, and to go to the movies or have dinner. As we learn to enjoy one another again as companions, our sex life is getting better, more spontaneous and relaxed.

Michelle: Romantic nights

After Lionel and I were reconciled, he really courted me. He was very romantic. I would come home at night and find music was playing, candles were burning, and pillows on the floor beside a bottle of wine. I felt like a beautiful young woman. What made his courtship so wonderful was that I actually had missed much of that as a young woman because of my illness.

Lionel's just being home all the time was more important than the romance, however. When I hurt from dialysis, he was there to cuddle and hold me. Words cannot express how important it was to have someone to soothe the pain. It's all I ever wanted.

There were other changes in Lionel, also. He was more patient. That's not to say he never fussed, but when he did, he'd catch himself and smooth out. It was as if he was saying to himself, "I can't do Michelle like this."

Some evenings he'd stop me as I entered the kitchen and say, "You are not going to cook. We'll go instead to a nice restaurant with soft lighting."

This continued for months and still does to some degree. But when I got really sick again, Lionel must have gotten scared. When I wanted to die and ended up in the hospital, he was frightened and didn't know what to do. He backed off a bit.

Now, it is as if we are starting over again. It's like we just got married. He didn't want to face my death. I didn't want to face my life. But we are holding each other up now. We talk more honestly than ever before. It may not be as romantic, but it is deeper. This time, he has been there for me. He really has.

Marta: Notice Mom

Joe and I have gotten a bit better about saving time just for us. We've actually had a few dates this year. And we've discovered the children love it when we go out together. They get very excited about it. That realization has led us to be more open about our sexuality in front of them.

I cut my hair short recently. My hair had been long for most of my life. And like most men, Joe professed to like long hair on women. So the children wondered what he would say when he saw the "new" me. On this day, I had cut my hair shoulder length. Well, as Joe came in the door, the children surrounded him, telling him to "Notice Mom, notice Mom." Well, Joe pretended he didn't notice. So, Joe and I began playing this game. I sort of teased him, twirling in front of him and acting flirtatious. He played dumb. The children were going nuts. Finally, he came over and kissed me and said, "You cut your hair. It looks nice." And the children were in the background, saying, "Yes!" It was fun watching the children respond to our being playful and romantic.

Tamara: Intimacy at home

Love was the foundation of our marriage from the start. But we forgot how to play during our troubled period. We are still on a tight budget, so we can't play in the sense of going on honeymoon-type vacations. In fact, we don't really even make time for dates. Occasionally, our son spends the night out. That's the only time we might go to a movie alone. But I am so glad to see Phil involved and productive again.

Even without dating and play, our sex life is the best it has ever been. In the past, sex just didn't work for me. Mostly, I thought, "Well, it's been a while since we had sex, so I guess I should do this," when Phil approached me. Now, we make love. I feel loved. I feel so incredibly loved. I *want* sex. I've never had that feeling before . . . ever. The better we are doing in other areas of our life, the better our sex life is.

With harmony in the home, laughing is easy. Joy is always right there. Sex just follows naturally.

Loving with Laughter
Humor dispels anger, hurt, fear, and stress. It is the candy of the soul.

Joan: Watch the bones

I was on a roll. In a bad mood, I was really haranguing poor Allen, issuing one complaint after another.

"Why didn't you . . ."

"You don't . . ."

He took it without comment for a while, continuing to dress quietly for his upcoming day.

Then he walked out of his dressing area into the bedroom. He spread his arms wide and with a big grin said, "Try to miss the bones as you hammer in the nails."

I had to laugh. And that broke the spell. With good grace and humor, he had made his point. I was being a five-star grinch.

The impact lasted for longer than that one moment. Whenever a bad mood, or fear, or other negative emotions would lead me to criticize Allen, I remember that morning. I laugh silently and keep my mouth shut.

Reba: Flap your arms

My mother gave me a great gift—the gift of laughter. Even though she is now eighty-seven years old, we still handle life's challenges with humor. My mom has some difficult health problems. But it is important to her to live in her home, and I've tried to help her stay independent.

She has a heart condition and is not supposed to do any physical work. This is a tough assignment for her. I would go to visit and find her out raking the leaves. She would protest that she "just did a little at a time. Nothing much." I wanted her to quit. I knew she was in dangerous territory, ignoring the doctor's orders. One day, I drove up and she was in the yard again, raking leaves. We talked a minute about how hard it was for her to quit doing those chores she loved to do. That was the bad news. But I said, "The good news is, when you don't want to live any longer, you just flap your arms really hard."

We both laughed and laughed over the image of Mom standing there flapping her arms. But she also got the point. She promised not to rake any more leaves.

Love Life

Gratitude Counts

"When you are thankful for what you have, you become fit to receive more. God is constantly pouring forth more blessings than we can possibly receive." These words of wisdom came from my mother. Being grateful brings love into our life. Thankfulness fuels the flame of love.

When I asked the seven women what they were grateful for, the list was endless. Tears filled their eyes as they talked of the positive changes occurring in their lives—restored relationships, new friends who had helped them through change, a renewed sense of self, an inner peace, a serenity in their lives.

But gratitude encompasses the small spots in our life also—the ten pounds Marta lost after she started to exercise, the neighbor who volunteered to take Joan's daughter to practice when she was ill, the adored pet who sits by Reba's side as she reads at night, the child who left a note saying "I love you" on Tamara's desk, the hug Michelle received from a friend, the serenity Sarah experienced as she drank her morning coffee and listened to the birds joyfully greet the dawn. Every day is filled with love if we but open our eyes and see it.

But my favorite expression of gratitude came in a note from Kate over my E-mail one morning.

Kate: Gratitude for the termites

Kate wrote: "Most people know that spring has arrived when the first crocus pushes up through the frozen earth, when the first robin grabs a worm, when a hint of green shows in the bare trees. I know spring has arrived when the termites first swarm in my kitchen.

"Today I am grateful:

- That they always swarm in the kitchen and not in my bedroom where that brand-new furniture probably looks pretty tasty to a hungry bug;
- That even though they may be in the walls all year round, they only make a visible appearance in March;
- That even though they fly when they swarm, they lose their wings

once they mate (which appears to happen in the first ten seconds!), so I usually only have to sweep them off the floor and not my countertops;

- That termites don't bite cats, nor does the cat bite them;
- That it takes a *long* time to eat a whole house;
- That I still have another year of termite warranty, which doesn't seem to scare them much at all!

"When the termites came this year, I think I reacted with grace and dignity. Before, I would have thrown myself on the bed and cried. Life is improving!"

Choose to Live Your Adventure

For each woman, an underlying current of spiritual strength provided her with the faith to go forward and make new choices. Knowing ourselves, being in touch with our inner souls, made all the difference. A trust in God led to a trust in events. A trust in a higher power enabled us to let loose. A sense that a divine source was leading led us to listen more closely; first, to ourselves, secondly, to others. And a discovery that we are loved let us love others more freely.

Each of us achieved this in her own way—some through meditation, some through prayer, some through their church affiliations, some through a very personal search. Religion is not an easy subject to tackle. It reaches deep into our sense of self. There are as many different experiences of faith as there are people in the world.

But to present solutions without a recognition that growth comes from an increased understanding of ourselves and our place in the world would be to trivialize that growth. For many of us, that understanding comes from a growing awareness of God, of a higher power that is directing. We can let loose, precisely because we are not the governor of the universe. The earth spins on its axis without our directing. Our individual lives, too, unfold before us as we let loose, listen, and love. These are the qualities that let us live our personal adventure to the fullest. We are free to follow that inner voice that says, "Take this path. It is your rightful place."

Choose to Love

There are infinite ways to love. Here are some discovered by the seven women:

- Take time for stillness, meditation, or prayer each day
- Receive giving from others
- Reward yourself for small successes
- Encourage others
- Give unconditionally
- Express gratitude
- Spend time with loved ones
- Find humor in small things
- Relearn to play
- Celebrate life

Your Story

Reflect on your answers to Questions 6, 7, 8, and 9 of the survey in Chapter One.

6.   I need:

7.   I don't need:

8. I enjoy receiving:

9. I find encouragement from:

What new things have you discovered that you need or don't need?

What can you do to receive more freely?

What new ways can you find encouragement?

What are some new ways you can love yourself?

How do you need to love others differently than you do now?

What are you grateful for today?

Reflect on your answers to Question 10 of the survey in Chapter One.

10.   I have no choice about:

*   Do you feel you have new choices?

Change happens one choice at a time.
*   What is one smart choice you can make right now to start your
    new journey?

Epilogue

This book has been a learning experience for all of us. We started out with more questions than answers. How did we become people who carry? Could we change? How do we change?

What began as an exploration became a journey of change for each of us. As we gained the courage to stop, listen, and examine our thoughts and actions, we found ourselves finding new answers. We were able to see what we had done, how we listened, how we loved, and how we expressed that love. Ultimately, that exploration led to insights on how and why we carry.

We recognized that to stop carrying is a choice. And making that choice is the first step to begin our change. But the solutions we explored weren't quick fixes. Nor were they without risk. But they were worth our efforts.

When I first made my decision to stop carrying, I felt over-whelmed by all the changes I needed to make. I was afraid of how these changes would impact my life and my business. But courage is feeling afraid and doing it anyway, so I jumped in with both feet only to find that I had taken on too much change at one time.

I discovered that change is a day-by-day journey. It happens one choice at a time. But I needed something to help me make smart choices each day rather than trying to do it all at once.

I developed an acronym to help me as I navigate my daily decisions. I've used it as the basis of numerous workshops, and have found it has helped others as well.

Quite simply, I live each day with CHOICE:

C   stands for   *Consciousness*

Smart choices are conscious choices, not doing things by default. I live in the present moment so that I readily see daily opportunities to make smart choices.

H   stands for   *Humor*

I look for humor in every situation. A willingness to laugh at myself and laugh with others dispels the tension in any situation. It illuminates hope and dispels my fear as I step into new territory on my journey through change.

O   stands for   *Options*

Every time I make a choice I eliminate other choices. But I recognize that I always have options. To do nothing is an option. To react rather than act is an option. Sometimes, the options are all attractive. Still, I must choose to try for the best and let the others go.

I   stands for   *Intuition*

I listen to my intuition, that quiet voice inside me that tries to get my attention but often fails. My inner voice helps me make the best possible choice. It protects me. When facing a choice I ask my intuition, not my intellect, "Is this really right for me?" The answer has saved me from a lot of tough lessons learned the hard way.

C   stands for   *Calm*

Calm is the quiet place where I go to listen inside. Even if it is in the corner of a crowded room, it is a refuge of renewal and insight.

E   stands for   *Experience*

Experience is a testimony to my past successes. This powerful resource gives me insight and tells me how to deal with life's daily challenges. Drawing on the strengths that helped me in tough times before, celebrating past successes, and trusting God with my future give me the confidence and courage to make new, smart choices every day.

I hope that your journey through this book has helped you become more aware of the opportunities for CHOICE and change in your own life. This book is not a to-do list to add to your already busy days. It is my hope that you will take the ideas offered here and adapt them to create your own map to a more loving, fulfilling life.

ABOUT THE AUTHOR

Hattie Hill, chief executive officer of Hattie Hill Enterprises, Inc., is a businesswoman, entrepreneur, professional speaker, and international management consultant who works with companies in Europe, South Africa, the United States, and the Caribbean. She is considered an expert on women's issues, global leadership, customer service, and diversity.

Hill was one of the top "Forty Under 40" Dallas business and community leaders honored by the *Dallas Business Journal* in 1994. *Dollars and Sense* magazine honored Hill as one of its "Best and Brightest Business Women," *Successful Meetings* magazine named her one of its "Hot 25 Speakers," and *Mirabella* named her one of the leading "Women of the Future."

Hill has been a columnist for *Meeting News* magazine and is frequently quoted as an expert, most recently in *The Wall Street Journal* and *Black Enterprise* magazine. The author of *Women Who Carry Their Men,* Hill lives in Dallas, Texas.